e College   LIBRARY

Learning Support Assistants
and their work

UNTOLD STORIES:
Learning Support Assistants and their work

edited by Tim O'Brien and Philip Garner

Trentham Books

Stoke on Trent, UK and Sterling, USA

Trentham Books Limited

Westview House	22883 Quicksilver Drive
734 London Road	Sterling
Oakhill	VA 20166-2012
Stoke on Trent	USA
Staffordshire	
England ST4 5NP	

First published 2001

British Library Cataloguing-in-Publication Data
A catalogue record for this book is available from the British Library

1 85856 250 3

Designed and typeset by Trentham Print Design Ltd., Chester and printed in Great Britain by Cromwell Press Ltd., Wiltshire.

iv

Contents

Dedication

*For Learning Support Assistants everywhere...and for our children
Rosie, Mairídgh, Keir, Evangeline and Charlie, who continue to
teach us to listen closely...*

Acknowledgements.

Our work on this book would not have been possible without the support of a large
number of Learning Support Assistants, who we met during professional development and training sessions or who offered to assist us by telling the 'stories' which
comprise this book.

They include not only the individual authors of chapters, but also those LSAs who
took part in 'focus group' discussions in London, Bristol and Nottingham, and those
LSAs whose stories we were unable to include

We would also like to thank the schools in which our contributing LSAs currently
work:

Alexandra School, South Harrow. Middlesex
Cirencester Kingshill School, Cirencester
Hazelwood School, Aberdeen
Oldfield House School, Hampton. Middlesex
Perry Court Junior School, Hengrove, Bristol
St Barnabas C of E Primary School, Montpelier, Bristol
St Christophers Special School, Westbury Park, Bristol
St George's Priory PRU, Nottingham
St Stephen's CE Junior School, Kingswood, Bristol
The New School at Westheath, Sevenoaks, Kent
Woodstock Special School, Henbury, Bristol

Jane Tarr, Director of the Programme for Continuing Professional Development at
the University of the West of England, Bristol greatly assisted our data-collection
and supported us in other ways, as did Simon Kitson, Educational Psychologist with
North Somerset Educational Psychology Service.

Elsie Blackwell, Dianne Levey and Irene Dale, all at the Nottingham Trent University, assisted us with transcriptions and word-processing.

Finally, we'd like to say a special thank-you to our publishers for recognising the
importance of hearing the voice of Learning Support Assistants by commissioning
this book.

Tim O'Brien
Philip Garner

1

Tim and Philip's story: setting the record straight

Tim O'Brien and Philip Garner

An emerging idea

Chance meetings often create chances. Unknown to each other, we had both been invited to speak at a conference in Dublin about eighteen months ago. The work of Learning Support Assistants (LSAs) was not a topic at the conference – but it became a focal point in our discussions over the course of the ensuing weekend.

We discovered that we both had a sense of disquiet about the way in which LSAs were seen as being pivotal to the development of successful inclusive practice. Many LSAs we know had expressed anxieties about their low status and low pay, their lack of training and the complete absence of any identifiable career path or structure. In our conversations, we began to ask questions about the varied nature of their role, what their experience was, and how their contribution to a child's learning and personal development differed from that of a teacher – if it did. As our discussion continued we began to identify points of similarity in our thinking about the vital work that LSAs do and the conditions under which they do it. Amongst these were: their potential marginalisation within the adult communities of schools; their frequently tenuous contractual situations and their woeful rates of pay – all of which belie the importance of the work they do, often with children with some of the most challenging and complex learning needs. Reflecting on their conditions of service, we posed a question: What is the difference between an LSA and a parking meter outside the University of London's Institute of Education? The answer – about one pound an hour!

But our conversation was *about* LSAs rather than *with* them. As is often depressingly typical of gatherings of academics and teachers, there were no LSAs at the conference who we could invite to join us in our musings. This in turn triggered a line of thought which led to an admittedly subjective critique of some of the things that have recently been written about LSAs and their role. Both of us felt strongly that here was another classic case of a group of 'workers' – a largely female group too – being 'done to' by others who were perceived as being in positions of greater authority and knowledge and therefore able to exercise power over them. The realisation that we might be reinforcing this situation, through the discussion that we were involved in, made us feel very uncomfortable, especially as neither of us had ever worked as an LSA.

We then began to consider some of the published material about LSAs that we had come across. As a general rule, this seemed not to incorporate the views, expectations, aspirations, beliefs and values of LSAs themselves, nor any of their critical reflections on the job they were engaged in. Subsequently, our discomfort was heightened when re-visiting some of this material during our preparatory work for *Untold Stories*. We became even more aware of how the language used in these texts appears to be the language of domination, manipulation and exclusion – for instance, one author advises that LSAs should be '*used* (our italics) properly and well', whilst more than one official document talks of 'utilising them effectively'. It was as if we were reading the instruction manual for a useful household tool, rather than discovering how LSAs and teachers might best work together in a professional partnership aimed at improving the quality of learning, and quality of life, of the children they work with.

There is a serious danger that the 'voice' of the LSA will continue to remain never much in evidence. In some cases it might be 'listened to' in school staff meetings – and there are LSAs who are now taking active roles on school governing bodies. But there is, in particular, a voice vacuum for LSAs, especially at conferences dedicated to discussion of their role, and in the proliferating number of books and articles written about them. And yet we were in danger of reinforcing this very situation ourselves.

Our discussions over the course of those two days in Dublin weaved from one topic to another, but we kept returning to LSAs and their work, such was our belief in their intrinsic importance. Both of us have worked in schools as teachers and more recently as practice-based researchers; during this time we have had the good-fortune and privilege of working with some outstanding LSA colleagues. Whilst working in schools we have also heard first-hand accounts about their achievements in supporting children with learning difficulties. These observations and commentaries were representative of a broad range of backgrounds, aptitudes and experiences. Quite apart from their positive engagement with the children and young people they were supporting, it became clear to both of us that one of the principal defining features of these LSAs was their capacity to make us think about our own practice so that it could continually improve. In other words, they were partners in a meaningful, formative enterprise rather than having a walk-on part in an educational drama (or in some regrettable cases being employed simply to paint the scenery). Moreover, these LSAs showed us the importance of enabling children to think in a more focused way about their learning. They do this in many ways, for instance by: modelling positive behaviour, establishing and developing relationships, increasing learner confidence and self-belief, encouraging risk-taking – in fact, empowering the learner.

Returning to our parking meter analogy, we are tempted to speculate what fee an educational consultant would charge to undertake all of the work of the type we have described – and the skills and expertise it encompasses. LSAs provide an essential contribution and yet the current level of their pay diminishes their status – as it does their opportunity to inform strategically what goes on around them. This is an indication of the reality of their experience in schools – doing pivotal work, whilst being poorly paid and often unacknowledged.

LSAs do not comprise a neutral canvas on which these conditions are represented. Successful LSAs we have worked with show themselves to be people who have strong commitment and emotional connection to those they work with. Nor do they constitute an un-skilled and un-thinking work-force, to be deployed when times are difficult or for the convenience of 'the system'. Like many others involved in special educational needs, they have strong and principled views about many aspects of the work they do. Consequently, they are a resource which should not be ignored or demeaned either by classroom teachers or by senior managers and others. Their status as people who support and develop learning has to be raised. During a recent course an LSA who works as a member of a behaviour support team, visiting different schools to support children in danger of exclusion, told us how one simple adaptation had changed how others perceived her. She would arrive at a school to support a child, wearing a badge that identified her by name and by occupation – 'Fola, LSA, Behaviour Support Team'. Even though she was also a trained counsellor, she talked of some teachers being dismissive of her and of what she might be able to do to help a child who was experiencing emotional and behavioural difficulties. How could an LSA carry out such an important and complex job – especially when some teachers were finding it difficult to do? The fact that she was also a trained counsellor was never brought up in conversation.

Unfortunately, this experience was not peculiar to one school; it happened in many. Fola decided that she would alter the 'job title' on her badge. Her new badge said 'Fola, Education Department, Behaviour Support Team'. She talked of being afforded much more professional respect when she wore this new 'label' and of being asked for theoretical and practical advice by teachers. She was also able to talk about her training as a counsellor. It was on the same course that we met an LSA who worked in a school where LSAs were still not 'allowed' to spend time in the (teachers') staffroom. Although these anecdotal examples cannot be generalised to all LSAs, they do raise questions about their current role and status.

National discussions have been taking place in England regarding the future role of LSAs over the last two years – a brief overview is provided in the second part of this chapter. New guidance on their 'function' and work patterns has been forthcoming, which is supportive of the rhetoric that LSAs *are* important people. The sobering reality is that many of these discussions do little to model processes for social inclusion and still less for enhancing mutual collaboration with LSAs themselves. Consequently LSAs have no say in making decisions concerning what happens to them. They may also be excluded from discussions about what should happen to individual children of whom they might have a more intimate knowledge than anyone else in the system. Even more distant, it seems to us, is the prospect of their being meaningfully included in any strategic planning of provision at a regional, or even national, level.

Past accounts of the work of LSAs, be they from a theoretical or managerial standpoint, have largely been provided by those who are very far removed from the day-to-day experiences of LSAs in the classroom. Before leaving Dublin, we resolved to explore the possibility of providing a forum for LSAs to tell their own tales – stories that have previously remained untold. To us, this possibility seemed to be best explored by presenting the voices of LSAs in a book. In compiling this series of stories from LSAs, we wish to adopt a forthright position. So, although we have been entirely responsible for identifying a group of LSAs who were prepared to 'tell a story', and for any interviews and transcriptions that have resulted from their doing so, the book you are reading most properly belongs to its contributing LSAs themselves. The stories are *theirs*, they belong to them, and are presented in their original words and, we very much hope, without any (additional) academic violation. Over fifty thousand words – and only a handful of references! Outside the substantive part of the book we do, however, provide the reader with a brief account of how these stories came to be told.

We do not wish to position ourselves as two commentators who seek to disparage existing research traditions. We earnestly believe in a fundamental need to report 'truth' and we accept that there are various ways of constructing, classifying, representing and legitimising 'truth'. However, we seek to assume a stance, increasingly celebrated by many in educational research, which recognises that empowerment of the 'researched' is the most potent (ethical?) position to adopt – even though at times there might be compromises to preserve the integrity of an informant's 'voice'.

We believe that this book can be seen in a number of ways. It is, hopefully, a forthright statement as well as being representative of a growing tradition of emancipatory writing and research. It can be seen as emancipatory in many ways: for example, it validates the voices of LSAs whilst at the same time encouraging and authenticating self-enquiry and challenging stereotypes. Critiques of each story are left for individual readers to develop. We do not see our role as to provide a critical superstructure – in terms of either an introductory context-setting or a summative drawing together of the theories and themes embedded in this collection of compelling biographies and reflective accounts of real lives in the real world.

It is our belief that the slightest hint of the stain of 'academia' will corrupt the potency of the message being carried by these stories. Moreover, we strongly believe that it would be disrespectful to the authors concerned: as 'academics', we could be implying that our technical rationalisation of their stories is an expanded version of 'what she or he really means to say...'

We do, however, offer some points for reflection and action at the conclusion of each chapter. We believe that these are not invasive. They do not seek to challenge the authenticity or validity of what the LSA has written. Nor do they present our views of the emancipatory knowledge that has arisen out of the research process. Rather it is our hope, and anticipation, that the points we add as a coda to the narratives contribute to their status. During the process of developing our summary points it occurred to us that one of the benefits in so doing was that the composite set of 'points' provide a useful antidote to the instrumentalism that seems to pervade much of the 'training' that LSAs are encouraged to undertake. The stories from the LSAs suggest that they think and operate very much in the tradition of the reflective practitioner.

In a very real sense, therefore, this volume belongs heart and soul to the LSAs – so much so that we are already diffident at being viewed as the book's editors, a word which can carry inferences of a dominant and selective approach to what might be 'acceptable' to the reader. It may also appear to reinforce, and be implicated and engaged in, the models of exercised hierarchical power we have already expressed concern about. These Untold Stories, then, belong quite properly to the LSAs who are their authors, and stand as both a tribute to their work and a message to decision-makers. LSAs have principles, ideas, skills and sometimes, as described by one of our contributors, a 'superhuman' commitment to their work. Their voice needs to be – has to be – heard at the very heart of the policy-making machine.

Scene-setting for the stories

Our own account would be incomplete – and many readers' understanding of these collected untold stories rendered less potent or intelligible – if we ignored the recent dramatic changes in educational policy impacting on the work of LSAs in the British Isles. Accordingly we provide a broad-brush sketch of some of these most recent developments, identifying their key features and pointing up some of the practice-related issues that appear to resonate in the narratives and meta-narratives of our contributors. We have sought to present an analysis which is in keeping with the substance and spirit of this book. In other words, we offer an impressionistic and personalised sketch of some of the key policy- and practice-related themes affecting LSAs, whilst leaving to others an in-depth discussion of underpinning issues of power-relations, management, gender, educational inclusion, decision-making and so on.

The increased importance given to LSAs in recent years has its origins in the Green Paper, *Excellence for All Children: Meeting Special Educational Needs* (DfEE, 1997) and *Meeting Special Educational Needs: a programme of action* which followed it (DfEE, 1998). Also in 1998, another Green Paper, *Teachers Meeting the Challenge of Change* (DfEE, 1998b) indicated the likelihood of a rapid increase in the numbers of LSAs in schools. Many would be supporting children who encountered learning difficulties. LSAs have come to be seen as integral to the effective learning of children who have special educational needs and to their fuller inclusion in schools. Thus the official version is that 'Learning Support assistants play an important role in supporting pupils with SEN and in helping to make inclusive education effective for them'(DfEE, 1999). It goes without saying that the unofficial version might be radically different if it were written by LSAs themselves and analysed how this 'important role' works in practice.

At present estimates vary as to the numbers of LSAs involved – the Centre for Studies in Inclusive Education (CSIE), for instance, suggests that in mid-2001 there were over 80,000 LSAs in mainstream schools alone. Central government has promised a further 20,000 full-time posts by 2002.

This expansion is being accompanied by widespread developments, both nationally and more locally, offering guidance to schools regarding the induction of LSAs and their subsequent role. Training emphasises behaviour management, curriculum support (especially in literacy and numeracy), as well as wider issues relating to the context of schools (DfEE, 2000a). In addition, a consultation exercise has been undertaken on a set of good practice guidelines for LSAs (DfEE, 2000b).

Recent years have also seen a sharp increase in the number of theoretical critiques, 'good practice' manuals and training packs. Balshaw (1999) produced a set of training materials for teachers and LSAs, for instance. Whilst being inclined on occasions to use the same dominant linguistic forms against which we have previously railed, the book commendably signalled the need for whole-school training, in which teachers explored the vital questions of pupil support in collaboration with LSAs themselves.

Accompanying these commentaries, Farrell, Balshaw and Polat (DfEE, 1999), in work commissioned by the DfEE, identified a number of key findings from a national study of the role of LSAs. Amongst the issues that they raise – and with which readers of this book will find powerful parallels in the storylines of its contributors – are:

•   little consistent pattern of working practices within and between mainstream and special schools

- the need for a single 'profession' of classroom assistants with a unified career structure
- the lack of planning time for LSAs and teachers
- enthusiasm and commitment of the vast majority of LSAs to their work
- that LSAs mainly felt supported by senior management and part of the whole school team
- that LSAs were extremely concerned about their low levels of pay and almost non-existent career structure
- the need for a nationally recognised and accredited training programme for LSAs, linked to salary and career progression
- the finding that only 20% of LSAs would consider becoming qualified teachers.

These observations suggest that, whilst much has happened in recent years to refine and enhance the role of LSAs, there are numerous issues which remain as matters of concern and tension. Listening to what LSAs have to say helps illuminate these whilst at the same time providing some of the focal points needed for the development of a more inclusive approach to their inputs.

Points for Reflection and Action

- Are Tim and Philip's comments concerning the status and pay of LSAs still relevant, given recent developments regarding conditions of service for LSAs?
- Can any value be gained from the kind of storytelling that Tim and Philip make use of in this book? In particular, are they overstating the importance of these accounts in helping LSAs to reflect upon and develop their professional practice? Most importantly, do they provide others who are professionally involved in education with a clearer picture of the 'real world' of the LSA?
- Tim and Philip describe, albeit briefly, some of the recent developments in SEN which have emphasised the pivotal role of the LSA. Using this as one baseline, how do you see the future unfolding?

References

Balshaw, M. (1999) *Help in the Classroom*. London: David Fulton

Centre for Studies in Inclusive Education (2001) *Learning Supporters and Inclusion*. Bristol: CSIE

Department for Education and Employment (1997) *Excellence for All: Meeting Special Educational Needs*. London: DfEE

Department for Education and Employment (1998) *Meeting Special Educational Needs: a programme of action*. London: DfEE

Department for Education and Employment (1999) *Special Needs Update* (3). London: DfEE

Department for Education and Employment (2000a) *Induction training for Teaching Assistants*. London: DfEE

Department for Education and Employment (2000b) *Teaching Assistants: Consultation on Good Practice Guidance*. London: DfEE

Farrell. P, Balshaw. M, Polat .F, (1999) *The Management, Role and Training of Learning Support Assistants*. London: DfEE

2

Louise's story: making connections

Louise Fenlon

As a child I never really enjoyed school. The main reason was that, like many children, I had lots to worry about. There were problems at home and school just became an added pressure. When I was in school, I wanted to be at home. When I was at home I was thinking about the pressures of school. It was a vicious circle because, wherever I was, I was anxious about what was going on somewhere else. As a child you do not really see this as pressure, as it is your normal day-to-day life, but looking back there was a lot of pressure for me. For any child who has worries about what is going on at home, school can become an institution where you do not want to be at all.

When I was at primary school I just kept my head down, sat at the back of the class, and got on with life. My secondary school was a massive comprehensive. Home difficulties continued and I often found myself 'on report' in school. This did not really work, as it did not help me to deal with my worries. My family saw it as intruding into our business. The families of children who find school difficult can be protective of their children. They want to be seen as normal families, not trashy families, just because they might have a problem going on. All families can have problems and things that go home from school, like reports, should never make the families feel bad.

I would sit and look out of the classroom window and want to be away from school. I was attending school but inside my head I was at home. You do not have the skills to switch off when you are young. Monday morning would be horrendous as you had just dealt with a difficult weekend and now you had to go back to school. You just cannot see why exams and lessons are important and then you transfer it somewhere. Some people do it by bad behaviour. Some people do it by truanting. That was my choice: truanting. It is difficult to deal with when you are young and problems seem to escalate around you. It is scary and you lose focus. This is what it must be like for some of the young people I work with now. I attended other big schools, but eventually ended up attending a unit. It was very small. It focused upon getting the curriculum done and being self-disciplined. This was their way of helping you to deal with what was going on for you at the time. I'd have liked it if they had placed more emphasis on empathy.

My mother has been a big influence upon me. When I grew up I was very close to my mum. She is a loving, caring and strong person. She made me feel safe and she was always supportive. I would like to think that I show some of her qualities in the way that I do my job with young people who have emotional and behavioural difficulties (EBD). This is a connection that I can make now as I look at what I do and how I do it.

Becoming an LSA

I have done different jobs such as selling kitchens and selling fruit. I did enjoy one job I had working as a helper at a Montessori Nursery. I asked for some training so I could be better at what I did, because I realised that I like working with children. My current job just fell into my lap. I left south London and moved elsewhere. I had taken a counselling course and also an information technology course. I met someone who had been on the counselling course who told me about a job that was available at the school where I now work. I was interviewed for the job and was really happy to get it as a full-time job. My role has recently changed from Learning Support Assistant to Student Welfare Officer. In my new role, I induct the new pupils, take Information Technology (IT) lessons after school and run the IT club at lunchtimes. I also integrate new pupils into the school. Many of these pupils are described as being school phobic. When I first started at my school there were only two LSAs, and now there are twenty-five! This shows how much the school has grown and how the school sees a need for LSAs and how it values them.

LSAs and status

People often talk about status as an area LSAs may be concerned about. I find it hard to define status as it makes you look too much at the individuals. I prefer to think differently – about how people work in a team; how they can all work together to help the pupils. If teams really work well there is no hierarchy and everyone feels that they are working at the same level. In the classroom it does not matter who is the teacher and who the LSA because your goals are the same. If a child is upset, someone helps; if a child is stuck with their work, someone helps. The teacher and the LSA have to talk to each other regularly about the pupils and about what the teacher is teaching, so that this type of teamwork can happen. They can step back and talk about who might be the best person in the team to help a pupil. In this way you do not have to bother with status, just with who is the best person to help. With the pupils in my school you have to have a plan of what you are going to do. The trouble is that the plan might suddenly not work and then you have to make a different plan that relies on your instinct. Although it is instinct you also have to plan it to a certain extent.

I am confident in knowing that I can go to any member of staff, especially the management team, and stress any concerns I have or ask for advice. I know that I will be listened to and this is one way of feeling that you do have some status. The same applies to the pupils because every child has rights too and they need to be listened to. Finally as an LSA I am able to attend the same training days as teachers.

Making connections

One of the most important parts of my work is being good at making connections. In the classroom there is a team. The team is the pupils, the teacher and the LSA. They all make connections with each other.

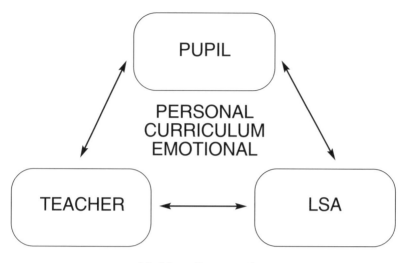

Making Connections

Connections are part of a relationship and are usually emotional. Connections depend upon things like experiences, mood and time. So one of our pupils may have been through something two years ago and it might not be affecting them until now. Maybe a bad dream could have caused them to be upset and to remember things they would prefer to forget. This will affect their mood. When this happens the LSA and the teacher have to change their levels of connection for that pupil. The connections between the LSA and the pupils might have to be much stronger on that day and the teacher reduces their connections. It may be that the connections with the pupil become much less as this might be what the pupil wants. The connections might have to be stronger at a curriculum level for things to be OK. It might be that connections have to be more regular at a personal or emotional level. When everybody is clued into making the best connections then you've got it sorted. It's like clockwork, with everyone working closely together.

We have to be aware that different connections work for individuals at different times. Words, actions or even a look on someone's face can trigger off emotions in our pupils. They can react to this and it can take weeks before connections can get back to normal again for that pupil. The LSA and the teacher have to work at making the best connections for the pupils and although clockwork connections might be seen as perfection by some people, I have experienced it. Like any relationship within a school, it all takes time and the best connections are always sincere.

I love my work. It is hard to define why I say that I 'love' the work, I just do. There are times when I feel like pulling my hair out and feel as if I can never go back. But the next day I just wake up and say to myself, 'right...new day, let's go'. I would say that every night I go home and think about situations during the day and then think about how I should have handled them differently and if that could have helped the pupils more. This is another part of the LSA job – you learn something new every day. I have never had two days the same. The times when I feel at my happiest in my job are when I see changes around me. For example, one of the boys might not have smiled for four days and then he smiles. You do not have to be involved, you might be walking by and see it happen and you notice it happening. You feel happy yourself because it tells you that he has taken a step, he is not feeling as bad as he did four days ago. It might be that another LSA or a teacher has made it happen, but it still makes me feel good. It might be that it is another pupil that makes it happen, in the way that pupils do when they create their own support network. This is also to do with connections, because there are times when they need a friend to talk to who is not an adult. This way they can sort their problems together. So, if a pupil says 'go away and leave me alone', the adult has to think about doing that – as being left on your own to decide who you want help from might be the best way forward. Sometimes the connections can be affected when an LSA is called out of the lesson to help deal with a crisis. When they come back they have to get the connections going again.

Approaching your work as an LSA

To be an LSA you really do have to enjoy contact with children and young adults – feeling pleased for them that they are actually in school. What might appear to be the smallest things to someone from outside are really rewarding parts of the job: such as how good you feel when you receive a little card or note from one of them saying 'thanks for being there', or if they say 'thank you' for support you have given. It is these experiences that make you feel that it is natural to go the extra mile for them. You might not always get positive feedback but you just keep going, because, at the end of the day, nothing is ever too much trouble. That is how you approach what you do. Working as an LSA in an EBD school, you have to:

- take one day at a time

- be genuine at all times – the pupils know who is sincere and who is not

- be yourself

- believe in the children and their ability to be strong

- help the pupils to trust themselves

- be patient and calm

- do not take verbal abuse, lashing out or anger personally – the pupils are never angry at you, they are transferring it onto you from another area of their life. They may not have been taught any way of expressing their anger differently, and so there will be times when you get it directed at you. They can learn social and emotional skills from the way the adults act. We might not even think that they are watching us but usually they are. This means that you have always got to try your best to behave in a way that they can learn good things from

- be prepared to make mistakes and try not to feel guilty if you think you have let a pupil down.

- show that you have a sense of humour

- do not play at being a martyr. Nobody can solve everyone's problems. You have to know when to step back and allow someone else to take over or to give the pupils some privacy and space.

Working with individuals

There are many individuals I have worked with whose success stays in my memory. One boy had not been in school for a long time but had really wanted to attend – he just felt that he could not. He had a massive amount of determination and eventually was courageous enough to give it a real try. I feel proud for him now when I see him running around with his friends enjoying life, that is definitely a success. One little girl arrived very confused and unhappy and now she has grown as a person. Even though she is so young she is one of the kindest people I know. I remember another boy who was extremely withdrawn and unable to express himself when he came to the school and who is now a happy, confident boy who has made friends. He has made massive steps.

The Letter Writer

Out of the blue one day, I started to receive letters from one of the girls in the school. She used to be school phobic and would not talk. I had to think about what the best way was of dealing with this. I thanked her for her letters but told her I was not going to write back to her because I did not want to reinforce writing as the only way of communicating. I told her I wanted her to eventually speak to me as I thought this would be the best thing to aim for. We built up the basis of a relationship and friendship through her writing to me and then I explained to her that when people are friends and are not far away from each other, you do not have to write, you can talk together. Now she is interacting and she is talking and that is great to see. She still writes to express her worries and her feelings. She gave me a letter today. In it, she says that she is never going back to certain lessons and everyone should leave her alone. 'Everyone hates me'. This really is about her looking in the mirror and hating herself and then finding it really difficult to face up to the fact that lots of people in the school like her – so she turns it around and says that everyone hates her. We just have to keep on telling her how much we like her and then one day she will believe it. She has written at other times 'Everyone hates me, except...' and then listed some LSAs and teachers. That is progress. She finishes today's letter with 'You can write to me or talk to me about this'. Now she has more choices and options but I will choose to talk to her. The essence of her letters have not changed since she first started writing them but she now allows me to talk to her.

The embarrassing email

On one occasion I was supposed to integrate a young boy from another school into our school. I went to visit his school, but he took one look at me and ran a mile. After discussing it with both schools, we decided that initial contact with the student should be through email, using the headteacher's email address. To start with I would send general emails. But as we started to get to know each other I would send messages with pictures of his favourite TV characters.

After a several weeks this boy said he was willing to come to the school and meet this person who had been sending the emails. The meeting went really well and he started to make regular visits to our school. We still continued to send emails to each other, to keep things consistent. One day I was browsing on the web and found a website about his favourite TV character. You could send postcards to people from the site. I thought I had struck gold and I sent him a postcard. Here is a word of warning – never send postcards from the internet before checking whether your message gets re-written. The next day I had a phonecall from the headteacher informing what was on the postcard. The words 'To my honey bunny' still make me cringe with embarrassment, the rest of the message had to be censored! Luckily, the pupil never got to read the postcard and the headteacher laughed about what happened.

The boy who would not let go

One boy will always stand out in my mind. He had not long started at the school and was very shy and timid. I am not really sure when and where it started but one day he suddenly clung to my side and did not let go. I would have to try to get him off me so that he could go into lessons and he would cry if I left him. I was worried by this and agreed with my colleagues that this was not 'normal behaviour.' If I was honest, I was well and truly freaked out by it all.

So I started taking him to lunchtime activities that I thought he would like. At first he was reluctant to stay but after negotiating with him and promising to meet him at the end of lunch he began to stay for the activities. When he realised I would be there to meet him after lunch he began to go independently. I began to arrange to meet him at certain times, which enabled him to become more independent because he had the security of meeting me. He then began to trust me and realised that he did not need to be by my side every moment of the day for me to support him. I still see him and he will come in and have a chat to this day but it lasts for about five minutes and then he's off with his friends. Looking back I had never experienced this before and thought that in some way I was responsible for the situation. I now realise that he was using me as a type of security blanket because he was missing his mum and home. He was looking for someone to feel safe with while he felt insecure.

Hold your head up

I remember sitting in music when a new pupil came in. She stood out because she had such a pretty face, but she was holding her head down and was wearing a hat. I tried to talk to her but she just stared at me. So I thought that another girl in the class might get her to open up. She smiled but she still kept her head down. One day I found her crying and asked her what was wrong but she wouldn't answer. So I decided to ask a series of questions and told her that all she had to do was nod 'yes' or 'no'. We communicated like this for some time and we continued to build our trust in this way. As time went on she made new friends in the school. Then one day I found her crying and asked what was wrong and to my amazement she answered and started speaking to me. I suppose you could say that we had our first 'heart to heart'. I felt genuinely touched because I really thought it would take a long time before anything like this might happen. I look at her now, a vibrant, cheerful, popular, humourous young lady. She holds her head up and looks you in the eye when she speaks to you. She has many close relationships that she has built up since she came to the school.

There are group successes too. It is amazing to see some of the plays and shows the pupils are able to perform to large audiences. Some of these children could not talk to anyone when they first arrived at the school, some would find it difficult even to get out of their parents' cars to attend school. It is definitely an amazing success to see them singing and dancing on stage. There are more private successes too, such as witnessing the children supporting one another and looking after each other. You do not have to look too hard to find a success for every child.

Qualities of an LSA

One way of looking at the personal qualities of an LSA is to consider the people you work with who you think are good at their job. I work with some wonderful LSAs. They have different types of personalities. Some might be quite shy and reserved. Others might be very confident. One could be brilliant at helping a pupil with the curriculum work. Another might be really good at talking privately when pupils have worries. Another could have a sense of humour that just keeps everything going – when the pupils are down or feeling angry, she can get them to smile and relax. I do not think that one person can have all the qualities that are needed to be an LSA. You need a team because the pupils need to experience all aspects of humanity and it would be unrealistic to expect one person to have all of those qualities.

What the pupils say

As the pupils probably know more about what makes a good LSA than anyone else, I have asked some of them for their views. These are the qualities that they think important, written in their words:

- someone who has been through the same problems
- knowing ways to help you when you are angry or upset
- helping the teacher to keep the class calm
- understanding students on a personal level
- able to see things clearly
- able to be trusted completely
- friendly
- someone who knows where you are coming from
- cheerful, so that you can be cheerful back.
- treat you like young adults
- let you have your own mind

- that you can tell them stuff and they don't go into the staffroom and tell everyone else about it over a cup of tea

- a sense of humour

- that if they say they will do something for you – they do it.

All the pupils said that an LSA has to be someone you can trust. They also comment on how they like it if an LSA is willing to understand that sometimes the work they are doing is difficult. In my work I find that there are times when I might struggle with understanding some of the things being taught in a certain subject. I can turn this around to my benefit for the pupils. I can say that I find it hard and then we set about learning it together. You can learn to work with the pupils this way. It can sometimes gain their respect.

School phobia

My new role as a Student Welfare Office involves working with children who are described as school phobic. I really enjoy the integrating work that I do with them, helping them to settle in to a new school and get a new start. I believe that school phobics really do want to come to school but it is an illness that has built up in their minds so that they become physically unable to come into school. It is important to see it as like an illness rather than someone who just does not care about going to school. Often a school phobic and their family are extremely relieved when the school understands this as a kind of condition where the school can help. In my experience these children feel misunderstood. They feel that people do not believe them and think they are only being naughty or lazy because they do not want to go to school. In fact they get stomach-aches and feel sick and they start to sweat and their hearts pound and a wave of panic goes through their body at the thought of going into a classroom let alone actually making it into a school. That is what it is really like for them. I often think that they must have been feeling alone for a long time. One of the things I have had to learn whilst working with children who have a phobia is that they need someone who is understanding and patient. I remember one boy who would not get out of the car. It would take about half-an-hour to get him to open the door and he would put one foot out of the car and then tell us he couldn't do it. After a couple of weeks he managed to get himself into an empty classroom. Like other phobic children, if you show them that you are giving up, you are confirming every negative comment and action they have experienced in their school lives. He needed support and encouragement and for people to believe in him, he did not need people saying that he was lazy or a bad person.

Integrating new students can be quite a daunting task. I have integrated students from various backgrounds and have learned that you cannot do it in an exactly set way because each child is so different. The key thing is to build trust. This can be the most difficult aspect of the integrating process, as most of the children have been let down by adults in their life.

I can often be faced with 'So what makes you so different to the other people?' or 'What makes you think that you can come into my life and make everything OK?' I think that sometimes the children cannot really understand why we care, why we are taking an interest in them and giving them our time. In my experience it can take time and often one step forward and two steps back. You can begin to start the developing of trust but you must let them choose the pace.

Points for Reflection and Action
- The story Louise tells provides examples of what some of the pupils in her school think makes a successful LSA. What might the pupils in your own school say?

- Louise includes an illustration of how she sees connections being made in the classroom. In what way can the illustration assist you in clarifying how you see your own job?

- School phobia is one of the themes in Louise's story. How far can Louise's insights help an LSA to support other children experiencing difficulty of this kind?

3

Karen Stanton's Story: more than 'just a helper'

Karen Stanton

I am a Learning Support Assistant (LSA) in a school for children with learning difficulties and associated emotional and behavioural difficulties. I am married and have three sons aged ten, eleven and thirteen. I left school in 1981 and went to College to study for the Nursery Nursing Examination Board (NNEB) certificate. I qualified in 1983 and my first job was in the London Borough of Lambeth in one of their day nurseries. After two years I moved to work at a different day nursery, and took maternity leave to have my first child in January 1988. 1 soon had three children all under the age of three, so I stayed at home to look after them.

I have a niece who has Downs Syndrome. She enjoys being with her 'Auntie Karen' and so I have always been very involved with her. I would go on school trips with her and go to see her in school concerts. On some occasions my sister-in-law and I would swap roles – she would have the boys for me and I would spend time with my niece. Looking back, I suppose this was my introduction into the world of special needs. I was soon known as a visitor to the mainstream school that my niece attended. After this school, she went to a special school that was seen as being more able to meet her needs.

When my own boys were old enough to go to school, I was ready to return to work. I needed a job that fitted in with their school hours so working at a day nursery was out of the question. At the time I also fancied a change from nursery work. I joined a 'supply' pool as a Nursery Nurse for council-run schools. I said that I would work in either mainstream or special schools. What happened was that a lot of my work involved supporting children who had a statement of special educational needs (SEN): 'statemented children'. These children were mostly in mainstream classes. I discovered that I really enjoyed working with the children who had a statement – it was the challenge that I enjoyed. After a while it became clear to me that I wanted to work in a special school. I had been involved with a secondary age special school because of my niece. I did not realise that I would eventually end up working at its 'sister' special school.

Years later my own son, Ben, was statemented. He attends a mainstream school and has additional support for his individual needs. Ben was diagnosed with leukaemia at the age of three. He had treatment for two years and this involved many hospital stays for him. Six months after finishing this treatment, Ben relapsed. We then had another two-year fight for his life. He ended up having a bone marrow transplant given to him by his elder brother. So, to a certain degree, I do know what it is like to have a child with special needs at home. We had five years of stress and worry but Ben is still here to tell the tale and it has certainly made me a stronger person. It has also given me a small insight into what it must be like for a lot of parents who have children with special needs.

From NNEB to LSA

I had looked around for a permanent position within special needs education but there was nothing going. One day, this all changed when I was phoned and asked if I was interested in a part-time contract at the school where I currently work. At the time, it was a special school for children aged four to sixteen with emotional and behavioural difficulties (EBD). The school was trying to support some of their children in returning to mainstream school and my job would be working with one particular pupil who was on an integration programme. I went to meet the headteacher and had a chat with him about what my role would be. He introduced me to a young lad who towered above me – and I am 5 feet 9 inches! I remember thinking, 'Oh my god, I hope he doesn't have a wobbly ...and if he does, how will I cope?'. The school at the time was in the throes of change. It had been an all-age EBD school but was now becoming a primary school with an even wider range of needs. I knew that the young man I would be working with had learning and behavioural problems but I was ready for the challenge. I liked the school and decided to take this part-time post.

It seemed really strange for me when I went to support his integration at a local high school as I had been a pupil there myself. What was even stranger was that there were still some of the staff there who had taught me years ago. I supported this pupil for five months and then a full-time post at the school came up. A new teacher and a new LSA were needed. I applied for the post of LSA, was interviewed and was successful. I was then introduced to the teacher who had been given the teaching post – we hit it off straight away. We found out that we both wanted new challenges and really liked the school. That was four years ago now and what rewarding and challenging years they have been.

My role as an LSA was to work alongside the teacher in supporting the children in their learning. There was a lot of responsibility in this job. This seemed to me very different from mainstream school and from integration work where the teacher often saw you as *just* an LSA. That is what it had felt like to me at the time. This attitude of only being an LSA did not come across in my new job. We were very much a team and Nicki, my colleague, valued my ideas and contributions. One of the main things that really stuck in my mind when I visited the school was the good atmosphere and the friendliness of the staff. Everyone was made so welcome. As an outsider you would not know who was the teacher or who was the LSA when you visited a classroom – that was how outstanding the teamwork was. I was very pleased to be part of such a school team.

I felt then, and I still feel now, that when you choose to work with children who have special needs it is not just a job. It becomes much more than that to you. You need to be a certain type of person. The needs of these children can be so great, and they rely on you so much to help them that you have to be aware of their needs all the time. I do not think that you could do the job as an LSA just for the money.

The money could be a lot better but it is not the motivation for doing the job. You have to really want to be there because if you do not you will not give it your all. You have to give it your all every day because if you do not, it is the children who suffer. Most of them have had a rough ride in their short lives. The children did not choose to have special needs and neither did their parents choose to have a child with SEN. The school can give the parents a break for six hours a day. The school should also give the children six hours of quality time too. That sums up what my job is mainly about. I really enjoy going to work and look forward to the new and unpredictable things each day brings. Every day is different.

Behaviour problems

The first class I worked with was all boys. It was a small group and to some outsiders it might seem that it was far too small a group for two adults to work with, but we really did have our work cut out. We had a boy with Downs syndrome who loved to draw, who had an excellent sense of humour and a lovely smile. He also had behavioural problems. His behaviour was often very sexualised. He would continuously ask us to kiss his lips. Sometimes, when he thought we were not looking, he would make suggestive movements on the floor or against the furniture. At first we would react to him asking us to kiss him, and say that he must stop saying this, but our reaction seemed to make matters worse. Eventually we made a decision to ignore what he was saying and we carefully watched his reaction. We found that ignoring him worked and eventually he hardly said it at all. We spoke with his parents about the sexualised behaviour and worked together to try to stop it.

There was another boy who had Aspergers Syndrome. He was a very good reader for his age, could draw incredibly detailed pictures and loved writing stories. He had a habit of spitting from the back of his throat and sniffing loudly. He had worked out that this annoyed his classmates. To be honest, it began to irritate Nicki and me too. We used to try to ignore this behaviour as well. By watching his reaction to being ignored we worked out that we could reduce the amount of times that he behaved like this.

Another boy had attended a school for children with severe learning difficulties (SLD). He loved cooking and really enjoyed music. He did not get on with the boy who had Aspergers. In fact they seemed to wind each other up continually. His behaviour was very challenging but what made things even more complicated was that his mother behaved in a challenging way too – we saw her as a being far too over-protective of him. The school has link books so that there is always a daily link with parents. This boy's mother would write comments in the link book that we thought were sarcastic. It seemed that she would complain about anything and it was hard for Nicki and me not to take it really personally. We made big efforts to get on with this parent and eventually our approach worked. The boy has now moved on to High School but his mother still keeps in touch with me. The boy in the class who had Aspergers Syndrome was quite a bright child but his temper was unbelievable. When he flipped we all knew about it. He did not hit out at staff but he would hit out at his fellow pupils. To try to help him to stop doing this we spent a lot of time talking to him. You could ask him to think about his behaviour and try to help him to change in this way. As the year went on our class grew. It was still all boys and the range of needs became wider.

New arrival

When someone new arrives in a small group they can have a big effect. I remember feeling really apprehensive about one child coming into the class. I had been told that he was autistic. In class, he would hit out at anyone. He would also bang his head very hard on any object whether it was the floor, the desk, or a person close to him. There were times when he also made the most unbelievable noises. I remember Nicki and I talking to each other about how on earth we were going to manage him. The first few weeks were very tough but our perseverance and support for him paid off. This particular child soon learned what type of behaviour Nicki and I would accept in the classroom and what we would see as unacceptable from him taking his needs into account. We tried out different strategies for coping with his behaviour and changing it. It was certainly trial and error to begin with but our perseverance paid off and by the time the child left the school to move on we both felt that we had really achieved something. It was real progress. When he first started at the school you could not get him into assembly but over time he was able to stay throughout. He found change very hard to cope with, as do many of the children with special needs that I work with. I remember many different experiences with him...

The things we do

I remember a camping experience that involved this boy. There were twelve children in all and what a brilliant experience it was. I volunteered to share a tent with this particular child, along with another child and another adult. I said that I would be totally responsible for him through the night. His mum had already warned me that he did not sleep very well and was 'extremely restless'. Well, she was certainly right about that! By four the next morning he was ready to get up and start his day, regardless of the fact that everyone else appeared to be asleep. I remember thinking to myself... it is pitch black, we are in the middle of nowhere, everyone else is asleep – what am I going to do with him? I decided that it was best for him if we went outside. To my relief and surprise I could hear voices from a different tent. We ventured over there and three other children were awake too. The head of the school, Dennis, was also wide awake. He lives in the middle of nowhere and we were all camped out in his back garden! Dennis and I talked about what the children would like to do and what would be an exciting use of the time and we decided that we should take them for a walk. I remember thinking to myself ... hang on, it's only 4.30 in the morning and here we are about to go walking in the countryside with four children. My conclusion was that we must be mad.

We told one of the other staff that we were off on a walk and said which children were with us. As we were walking, one of the children decided that he could not walk any further and it was almost impossible to get him to budge – so guess what happened? Yes, it was piggyback time. He was by no means a small child. By the time we arrived back at camp it was about 6.30 in the morning and I felt totally exhausted. The day had only just begun and I felt that I had already done a full day's work.

I could not give in to this feeling so, to get over this exhaustion, I kept thinking about the boy's mum, who had not had a break through the night for years. I just hoped she was making the most of it right now, and with this in mind I carried on. It certainly made me realise that having the children for six hours a day is nothing compared to having them for the other eighteen! Parents of children with special needs have certainly got their work cut out. We should not forget that.

This particular parent had a very good relationship with Nicki and myself. At first she was very reluctant to let her child go but after lots of persuading and reassurance she agreed. This was great news because I feel that the child benefited tremendously and hopefully so did his mum – even though, for her, it was just a short break. I do feel that in a special school you really have to develop a closer relationship with parents, unlike parents from a mainstream school. In that way they can begin to trust you and the school.

Another child we took to camp was from a travelling family. Her mother said that Travellers do not necessarily like their children to stay away over night. We really wanted the whole class to take part in this trip, so, after endless telephone conversations, and lots of re-assurance and persuasion, the mother finally agreed. I told her that I was a parent and totally understood how she felt. I also promised that if her child became distressed in any way I would personally bring her home. The girl had a whale of a time and on returning to school she would continually ask when we would be going camping again. After this camping trip I sat back and thought to myself just how lucky I was to be part of the team at my school, a team that includes the children. What achievements had taken place for several of them in that thirty-six hours! This trip reminded me again that you have to be a certain type of person to work in the area of special needs. I think of myself as an easygoing person who is quite extrovert and flexible and you need these qualities as an LSA. The children's needs are complex and you have to be ready to respond to them.

Celebrating success

When you work in special schools you can have so many successes. I remember one day one of the pupils I had been working with for eighteen months finally wrote her name. For a long time, she had managed to master all the letters in her name apart from the letter 'e'. This letter gave her difficulties. Then one day I was working with a supply teacher who was excellent. Some supply teachers are very good but as an LSA your experience of supply teachers means that you can meet some that are not so good and some that do not earn their money at all. If you have worked with a supply teacher who has not prepared any work, or has made no effort during the day, it makes you feel like saying that the LSAs should just run the class if a teacher is ill. Why? They know the children, they know the routines and they can help the day to run successfully and smoothly. When you consider what it costs a school to have a supply teacher for the day, good LSAs running the classroom makes more sense than employing a supply teacher who does not work hard enough. It can be a nightmare.

Returning to this excellent supply teacher. He gave me a strategy to work with which he felt would end up with the child being able to write the letter 'e'. He was experienced in SEN and he used to try out different methods. His interest was in the way the brain worked. To begin with I had to work on the figure 8 sideways – encouraging the child not to take her pen off of the paper at all. I was not convinced about this but thought I had nothing to lose so I persevered for several weeks. Eventually, having worked on this strategy, I asked the child to the write me a letter 'e' and after a few attempts she succeeded. Now the challenge was to get her to write her whole name independently – a task we had been working on for some time. Again, perseverance paid off. One morning the child sat down and wrote her whole name. When Nicki and I saw her do this we started dancing around the room because we were so happy for her. The children were just staring at us. The child was so pleased with herself. I took her into every classroom in the whole school, showing everyone what she had achieved. The other children were so pleased for her too and she got loads of stickers for her effort. Staff that had previously worked with her could not believe what had happened and one member of staff was so overcome by what she had done that she asked for a photocopy of the work to keep. What an achievement it was. This is what my job is all about and is one reason why I love it.

Extending my role

The role of an LSA is complicated. As well as teachers, pupils have perceptions of what your role is. One day Nicki and I were talking about a pupil's work and this particular pupil said to me 'Karen you are just a helper aren't you? Nicki is the teacher.' I was quite taken aback and explained to the child, 'I am a Learning Support Assistant and I work alongside Nicki. Nicki is the teacher but I am involved with teaching and learning too.' I did not like to be thought of as just a 'helper'. I had worked hard to get my NNEB and was proud that I had it. I was proud of my work in the school. This comment came up from this pupil on several occasions. One day I was in the class and this same pupil ran over to me and was really excited. She explained to me, 'Karen' she said, 'Nicki is not here right now, so now you are the teacher'. It's strange, because up until this point I had never really considered what the pupils thoughts on what my role or job were, or how they would interpret job titles, but this particular child obviously felt that there was a very clear dividing line. I did not feel that she respected Nicki any more than she respected me, and she would listen to both of us when we were supporting her with her work. She just seemed to think that all I did was 'help' and I suppose I just did not like being called a helper because I do so much more than that.

Recently I took on another role in the school as a Governor representing the non-teaching staff. Taking on this role gives me more involvement in the school and greater insight into what goes on behind the scenes. I applied for the post when it became vacant because I felt it important that there was someone in school to represent the LSAs. I was quite surprised initially at the different roles that Governors have. I have taken on the role of Numeracy Governor and I am also part of a team of four involved in organising and monitoring the school budget. This is all very new to me but already I am enjoying the challenge. It's amazing what a 'helper' can actually get involved in.

Very soon after becoming an LSA at my current school I trained to be a trampoline coach. I did this because we used to take our class to the local leisure centre for lessons and I felt that it would be good if the school had their own person who was geared up and qualified for teaching children with SEN how to use the trampoline. I also felt that the children would respond better to someone they already knew and that this would give them more confidence. It can be pretty scary on a trampoline, especially with someone you are unsure of. I was fortunate enough to be able to use a local high school's trampoline to take my class and to give them some coaching. This was a great experience and every child that I took really loved it. We have looked into buying our own trampoline for use in school but unfortunately the ceilings in the school hall and dining hall are far too low.

That's something that even an LSA cannot change!

Points for Reflection and Action

- Karen talks about a very positive working relationship between herself and her classroom teacher. What in your own experience are the factors that contribute to a successful working partnership? Are there any similarities between them and those in Karen's story?

- Karen tells us something of her work outside the formally recognised 'curriculum'. Who do you think benefits from this kind of involvement – in her story and in yours?

- It is clear from Karen's story that she works with children with a wide range of complex needs. She has thought a lot about how these needs can be met. How can LSAs working in similar situations best be supported in meeting complex needs?

4

Chris' story: looking inside my head

Chris Nicholas

It is never easy to start a piece of writing: the first sentence is always difficult. I'm tempted to begin with 'once upon a time'... but that's another story. So where shall I start? Who am I? Why did I become an LSA? ...Here goes!

My name is Chris, or Christine to my mother. I am 44 years old. As a child I loved school and stayed on until the sixth form. I wanted to teach but at seventeen a lack of confidence or belief in myself held me back. I applied to college and a bank at the same time. The job offer in the bank came before the college offer, and I took it – my decision was as simple as that.

I left school with a handful of GCSE 'O' levels and several more CSEs and went forward into the world of stocks and shares. I married at twenty one and at thirty had my first child, which changed my life completely. When she started school I couldn't wait to help, so I became a parent helper and since then have experienced many different teaching techniques. I got my first job as an LSA by luck. My daughter's teacher recommended me; we had got on well, so I was offered the job. It was only three hours a week but it was like coming home: a bit 'naff', I know, but it's true.

I now have two children: an eleven year old son Jack, who's in Year 6 and wants to be a builder like his dad, and a fourteen year old daughter Kerry. She is in Year 10 and has just started her GCSEs.

She's brilliant at music and wants to teach and I'm sure she will. I'm very proud of them both and it's the experience I've gained from these two that I hold in such high esteem. It helps me to understand and deal with other children's problems and insecurities and enables me to identify adolescent changes and progression.

Getting to know Robert

I suppose, if I'm totally honest, at first I thought the job would be convenient: school holidays, local, not too challenging, almost an extension of being a parent helper. But I soon found out how demanding the role was and I really did enjoy the challenge. The boy I first worked with fascinated me, and the more I got to know him and see what made him tick the more I wanted to try out my own ideas. In my account I refer to him as Robert. I thought I could see different ways of helping him to learn. I had taken psychology as an extension to my unfinished sociology 'A' level and wished now that I'd completed the course.

Robert and I moved up to the junior school together. A year later he was diagnosed as being autistic. By now I was working 18 hours a week and was beginning to feel far more confident. I knew him really well and could anticipate when he was stressed, couldn't cope or was about to blow. I began to do some research about autism and collected lots of information. At about the same time I started to get support from Heather, who had taken on the case. She gave me so much practical information and useable strategies and this contributed to my understanding of autism itself, the way that Robert saw life and how I could help him. I spent the next few years almost interpreting everyday life for him, writing social stories to help manage his anger and frustration, and making resources that appealed to his kinaesthetic style of learning. My creative streak was stretched to the limit – and I loved it!

Looking back, I think the thing that has given me greatest satisfaction in my job was the successful completion of four years in junior school by 'my' lad Robert who is now described as a pupil having Asperger's syndrome. I was told that he couldn't cope with life in the juniors. It was anticipated he would last only a year or two.

34

These predictions were wrong. I saw him through four years and he left gaining level 4 in his English SATS. Robert and I became very close and I learnt so much from him and was reduced to tears when I was allowed to hug him on his last day – something he allowed only close family to do. I do miss him and his quirky outlook on life...

I am currently working with a little girl who has cerebral palsy and am just beginning to get to grips with her problems. Her learning is erratic and her self-esteem is at rock bottom; she gets little help or encouragement at home. It does not help having a perfectly healthy twin. She joined us because the junior section of her previous school was on several levels with no wheelchair access. When we first started working together she constantly talked about her old LSA and almost went through a grieving process. Recently, she told me she had almost forgotten about her now and loved her new school. That is the best possible reward I could have for doing this job.

Why do this job?

I have asked myself many times 'why do I do this job?' and every time I come up with a different answer. The most obvious response is that I like children, which I do (honestly!) but it is so much more than that. The children I work with give so much of themselves and are frighteningly honest. I find it very easy to talk to them and I love listening to what they have to say. Sometimes it is quite scary how much trust they put in me and it really hits home how comfortable they are with me when they call me 'mum'. I suppose part of me still wants to be a teacher, and each time I go on a different course I realise that I could have done so. That makes me sad.

At 44 I feel that it is too late to be anything more than I am. I do feel however that I am an important member of the team in school. We all support each other and the LSAs are always included in everything from INSET days and writing IEP's to social gatherings. Our knowledge about the children we work with is valued. Quite often we have a better overall picture of an individual child's progress and needs. Personally, I've never felt like a downtrodden classroom assistant! Yes, I've made coffee for the teachers... but equally they have made it for me.

We have an excellent SENCO at my school and we have weekly meetings where we can discuss any problems or successes and seek advice. She keeps us well informed about changes within the system that affect us and any relevant courses being offered. The school does seem to invest in our training, an obvious benefit to both me and the school. It is a shame that there is such poor recognition of our work when it comes to pay. So much is expected of us: we differentiate work, prepare work sheets, do planning and make resources. We are trained to contribute to extended work in both literacy and numeracy – all structured teaching approaches and input at a fraction of the cost of a teacher.

The instability of the hours can be worrying and the fact that, even if you have a job things become uncertain for you when a child with a statement moves to another school. This means that, on the whole, the job doesn't attract younger people or men. It is more of a second career, taken up by women like myself who became involved after having children. I think that's a bit of a shame, as it is a very worthwhile and rewarding job.

About two years ago the junior school where I work started sending the LSAs on different special educational needs courses. I was terrified at first. What if I didn't live up to the challenge? I enrolled for a year-long course and it was probably the best thing I have ever done. I found I loved learning again and discovered that there was so much to learn. As is always the case, this course was in my own time but it was paid for by the school. It gave me so much confidence and made me realise how much I made a difference and how much more I could do. I successfully gained my Certificate in Learning Support and felt rather like the scarecrow from the *Wizard of Oz*. That piece of paper meant I really did have a brain!

Making progress?

I am worried about education at the moment: the lack of funding, the shortage of teachers and the possible knock-on effect that children are not getting the education they need. But there are many positives. The literacy and numeracy hours are excellent and I must admit I have learnt a lot as I sit through many a lesson. Things have also come a long way in the special educational needs area since I was at school. I remember at junior school there were two classes shut away on the top floor of the school: these were for 'remedial' children. We had no idea what this meant. Did they have two heads or three eyes? When we were 'integrated' for a day I was almost disappointed to find they were children just like me, who looked like me, and (shock, horror!) we had all been playing together in the playground for years. One boy even lived in my street! No one wants to go back to that situation, and I think children benefit from being educated together. It makes them more tolerant and less afraid of people who are 'different'.

I hope you enjoyed the guided tour of my head, which has been at times serious and at others light-hearted. I do count myself lucky. I love working with children and I love the job I do. What more could I ask?

Points for Reflection and Action

- In Chris's story she raises issues about 'integration' and inclusion. In what ways do you think that an LSA is in a position to contribute to a more widespread inclusive practice? Should they be?

- Chris tells us something about how complex the life of an LSA can become. Her illustration of this provides the basis for the cover of this book. How would you illustrate, in a drawing-with-words, the work that you currently do as an LSA – or with an LSA?

- Chris expresses concerns regarding the direction in which the education of children with special needs is going. To what extent should LSAs be involved in this kind of discussion – and at what levels?

5

Judith's Story: entering the world of profound needs

Judith Moseley

The door to Class A burst open and in they came: six eleven year olds. Mark went straight to the class teacher, holding out his hand saying, very precisely 'Good morning Mr Smith'. He scarcely glanced in my direction – but he knew I was there. The rest followed noisily, Felix stamping his feet and constantly turning his head. Mary was issuing a sort of growling noise. Kerlin came in jumping on both feet and muttering 'Duh, duh, duh...'. Tom went straight to his chair, curled up on it and proceeded to rock. Lloyd entered, took off his coat, hung it on his peg and just sat down. I gazed around the class, experiencing a sort of sinking feeling. Never before had I had dealings with such a wide range of special educational needs. Would I be able to cope? Could I establish a reasonable relationship with these children? My previous class of 24 five year-old pre-schoolers in South Africa seemed like an easy option by comparison.

I had arrived at this school for children with profound and multiple learning difficulties (PMLD) simply because of a need for employment. The past thirty years had been spent in South Africa, most of them as a nursery school teacher. During that time a few children had come to the school with attention deficit/hyperactivity disorder (ADHD), dyslexia and co-ordination problems, or just general slowness in learning. Often these issues had not been identified before and only began to manifest themselves as the children attempted to cope with being one among many children in a school situation. I found working with these children both challenging and rewarding.

When I returned to England and saw a position as LSA at my present school advertised at the job centre I applied. To my surprise I was offered the job, even though I was woefully inexperienced with the types of profound needs I would encounter. These included autism, Rett syndrome (a syndrome where all reported cases have been female and which can be characterised by motor difficulties and the loss of previously acquired skills), global retardation and Angelmans syndrome (a syndrome which also affects motor development)

Proving myself

My family and friends gave me three to six weeks...! I accepted the challenge and now, eighteen months further on, I am still here, enjoying the work. And I think I have established good relationships with all the children I work with.

One of the biggest challenges for me was to learn to communicate with the children I was about to work with, as none of them except Mark and Lloyd have any speech. In my view this is made more challenging in that their use of speech does not appear to be associated with creative thought. Thus, Mark can answer questions but needs leading questions; otherwise he repeats the last few words. Lloyd has echolalia, Mark is able to read, Lloyd is learning to.

So how was I to communicate and help the children, who had little understanding of the realities of their world or how to interpret what they are feeling, or the concepts of anger, or the effects of their own low self-esteem? Small nuances of tone are one way. I was working with Ann who was not very impressed with what I was helping her to do! She was making grumbling noises which I ignored. She tried to bite me. Undeterred I continued, so she sprayed me with spittle – a sure way to get me to move away!

There are two main ways in which the school addresses this issue of non-speech: through the use of Makaton signing, and the Picture Exchange Communication System (PECS). I have to be honest and say that I have not witnessed a great amount of signing by any of the children, with the exception of 'Please, more, thank you, biscuit'.

When prompted, one child will sign 'Sorry!' However, the staff is encouraged to use signing for dialogue with the children. PECS appears to be more successful. It involves the child conveying their need by means of presenting a picture. The system is taught to the children in slow stages. It usually starts with something the child likes, often food, and they learn to give the card in order to receive the wanted item. Once they have grasped the concept another symbol is introduced and another choice has to be made. Although it may initially be slow going, perseverance pays off, and in time the children are able to convey their needs and wants. This extends to a fuller language, with pictures to represent, pain, or the toilet, or going to the shops, for example.

At the beginning of this year I was asked to split my time between Class A and Class B. The latter were a very different group of seven children, four of whom are in wheelchairs, and one is visually impaired; their ages range from seven to twelve.

The two groups are very different and require different styles of teaching. For instance, one class is physically mobile, the other not. What is the common thread? All these children have very special needs; all need a lot of help. For this reason the classes have two or three classroom assistants as well as a teacher, and in the classes I am involved with we take it in turns to work with each child as, with the exception of Lloyd and Mark, all need assistance to perform their tasks.

Before coming to this school I had compassion for what I termed handicapped people. Perhaps this was because my primary school was next to a school for children who were at that time referred to as spastic. We would see them at break times and some of the more able children would sometimes join us for sessions. Being placed in such close proximity to these children who had special needs, I wondered if I would cope. What about the regurgitation... the saliva... the smearing...? And then having to clean up everything! But after a while these unpleasant things fade into the background as the personality of the child comes to the fore, and these special needs children become special children who happen to need different things.

When asked about the job I do I once said 'It's great... I get paid to play!' Perhaps this sounds rather flippant but much of my work is using sensory equipment, taking children to our dark room, or soft room, or assisting with physiotherapy and the PECS training. It is definitely fun, but it is still quite intense work. It is not always easy to get the children engaged, and the results of our efforts are not readily apparent. The children's progress and particularly their successes are small, but significant. Like when Felix, who constantly turns his head and looks sideways, looked straight into my eyes for a count of ten seconds and he really 'looked'... Or the first time Mark came voluntarily to me to shake my hand...or when Kerlin handed over the correct symbol for a biscuit without any help.

Moving forward

The forward steps they take are very small but nevertheless they do take them and it is most encouraging. One day Class A went for a walk as part of our geography lesson about rivers and bridges. What better place to go than down on the river path under the Clifton suspension bridge? To get there we needed to walk down through a wooded area. The trouble is it had been raining for about two weeks, and to say it was muddy is an understatement. Mary protested halfway down and sat in the mud and refused to move. Kerlin slipped and landed on her knees. Lloyd just loved standing in the mud and didn't want to move. But we made it to the path! We now wanted to climb over a small wall. Though our children may be able to walk, climbing is a different challenge altogether! But between us and with a lot of mutual help and support all the pupils made it. We had juice and biscuits before returning to school, arriving back a very muddy and unkempt group. But what a wonderful morning of challenges met and overcome by our special children.

Moving to Class B presented me with the challenge of moving children to and from their wheelchairs, and assisting them to walk. To do this I needed to gain their trust. Now, three months into the year, I am able to assist them in this way. At the school we have a policy on manual handling, but some of the children have special manual handling instructions, particularly those in Class B. This includes details of ways of being assisted out of and into special chairs, assistance to walk short distances, and so on. This class has an added dimension in that after being a class of only non-walkers, two active, able walkers subsequently joined them. This has altered the tone and dynamic of the class, requiring greater differentiation in lesson planning. As a group of LSAs, we divide our time among all the children. This is beneficial to all, in that it provides variety for the children as well as the staff. As we work towards the targets for the children we support them on a one-to-one basis, or sometimes on a two (children) to one teacher ratio.

The school I work in follows the National Curriculum, alongside the philosophies and teaching ideas of Rudolf Steiner. At first I wondered how age-appropriate education could apply to these children, whose cognitive development was way below their chronological age: in some cases at pre-school level or below. But by simplifying the information appropriately, supplying plenty of sensory experiences, and setting realistic individual education plans (IEPs), a successful educational experience can be provided. The Steiner ideas aim to make the children feel rooted and aware of their environment; much use is made of music, art and movement within the taught curriculum.

The work I do as an LSA is physically challenging, requires lots of patience and an ability to meet the children at their point of need. Whether this involves it encouraging Mary to stand, or Ann to walk, or Kerlin to hold a pencil, the work is rewarding and satisfying. I think we all know that we are making some difference in the lives of these children.

Points for Reflection and Action

- Like Judith, many LSAs sometimes have to work in different classrooms in the same school. What challenges (and what opportunities) does this present?

- Judith talks honestly about some of the situations she has to deal with in her work. For instance, she graphically notes 'the re-gurgitation... the saliva...the smearing...' What particular attributes must an LSA develop in order to deal in a meaningful, productive and optimistic way with such eventualities?

- 'Would I be able to cope?' Judith uses this phrase to describe her fears as she began a new job as an LSA. What 'coping strategies' do you employ in doing your own work? From where (or from whom) do you draw support?

6

Spencer's Story: it's all about learning

Spencer Burke

My background is important in my professional work. When I was nine years old I was referred to a school for children with Moderate Learning Difficulties (MLD). The school also had an element of Emotional and Behavioural Difficulties (EBD) to it. While I was there I found it very difficult to adjust to the school and to learning. This might have been because prior to that I was diagnosed as being epileptic and this meant that I spent quite a lot of time out of school. I still do not know if I had some sort of dysfunction of the brain but I did find learning quite difficult.

Unforgettable experiences

There are many experiences of attending a special school that I remember but there is one that stays with me and always will. I was out in the playground one day, standing in a line. Somebody pushed me and it made me angry so I swore at them. A teacher heard what I said and grabbed hold of me, pinning me against the wall – so I swore at him as well. He dragged me all the way across the PE hall, up the corridor, and to an office. He took me into the office and screamed into my face 'Malad, Malad, Malad'. He was really shouting it at me. I did not know what it meant. I could make no sense of it and so I just broke down in tears. I did not know what this word 'Malad' was. The nearest word I could work out that he might be saying was 'Mallard' because it sounded like that. I was crying but he just kept shouting it at me. It really shook me up. I never talked to anyone about this experience but remember that, as a child, I honestly thought he was calling me a duck! Eighteen years later, when I started getting into the job I am in now, I realised that this was old terminology and that 'malad' meant 'maladjustment' or what would now be called 'EBD'.

The school itself helped me with my learning problems by using games with numbers and words. I also used cue cards to help with my spelling. A teacher showed me how to break words up and that was the first time I learned to spell *Wednesday*. I broke it up and suddenly I could spell it. I was about nine years old then and it felt incredible. These personal experiences give me an insight into the work that I do now. Around this time I was diagnosed as diabetic. There was a group of pupils in the school who used to bully – that is what they did. When they found out I was diabetic they used to call me names, particularly 'sweetbag', because I was unable to eat sweets. Two of the children who used to do that lived on the same estate as me so I got this bullying in and out of school. It really upset me at the time. Now, as a consequence, I feel very strongly about name-calling as a form of bullying and am pleased to work in a school where behaviour of this type is not allowed to become a niggling problem for a pupil. Of course bullying will happen in EBD schools but dealing with it consistently and quickly can put a stop to it. The same applies to physical bullying. In my work, I have spoken with pupils who are bullying others and told them that it happened to me when I was at school and I tell them what it felt like. I explain this to them to help them to change. I also do it to try to stop the problem before it ends in violence. When I was a pupil in a special school and was being bullied, my uncle told me to search out the biggest bully and to smack them square on the nose. I did this and the bullying stopped but I would not suggest that as a way of solving a problem and nor would I condone it. You have to find another way.

I attended special school for two years and then moved to mainstream. There were some good times but I remember being in certain remedial classes. I hated being known as remedial. I used to be taken out of English lessons to attend remedial classes. I never understood why. I used to make my own decision about this and not do as the teachers said. I would not go to the remedial class but straight to English instead. The teacher would find me and bring me back to the remedial class. The remedial class contained people with varying difficulties and problems and we were 'set' into that group. There was a 'top set' and there was a 'remedial set'. I did not have a choice to go to English lessons as the teachers said I had to be in remedial classes. Eventually, by what is now known as Year 9, I decided to truant. I truanted a lot. I missed out on coursework and in then end I felt as if school was not for me at all and I went on a long work experience with the Royal Corps of Transport in London. I used my practical skills and I loved it.

I do remember some teachers from that school who influenced how I do my own job now. In my secondary school there were no Learning Support Assistants in the classrooms, only teachers. I remember how these teachers behaved. One was in charge of Special Needs and got to know me well. She was very caring and also very careful. For example, when she corrected your work she made sure that you realised that she was not correcting *you* – she was correcting your work. She would never say 'That is wrong. You should do it like this'. She would say, 'That is a very good effort, but here is a better way of doing it'. What we say to children and how we say it is very important. She would always put things positively.

Discovering EBD

After I left school I did different jobs. I was a security guard and even in that job people comment on your spelling. I remember writing someone's name down and another security guard said, 'You've spelt it wrong'. I just said, 'No I haven't, you can't read the way I write'. I enjoyed working with children and was involved in outdoor education. I especially enjoyed working with children described as 'inner-city children'. On one outdoor education event I was asked to be an instructor for a group of children who were described to me as having 'EBD' and I enjoyed it very much. I found that these children really try to make adults react to them by their behaviour or what they say. They would swear at you or behave in a way that you did not want them to. My tendency in working with them was to ignore it if it was not going to escalate, or to try to divert it sometimes with humour. I did not get into arguments with them or get aggressive. There are times when a difficult situation can be turned into something positive. People commented that I had a real knack for working with children like these. It happened almost by accident that I found out that I really loved the challenges that they presented to me.

I recognised that these children, and children with EBD who I have since worked with, have learning difficulties like I had when I was at school. Finding something difficult to do or difficult to learn sets their behaviour off. The first problem is about learning and the next one is about behaviour. Being expected to get things one hundred percent right is tough – my own learning is still not one hundred percent right. I still spell things incorrectly but I can deal with it emotionally. I may even find myself in situations where the children might know more than me about something, but then again, anyone can be in that situation in any school. When the pupils see me make mistakes that can make them feel better. They can also see how I deal with it and what I do, like admitting that something is wrong. They can learn from watching how I react to finding something difficult. I have developed strategies and they can see them. For some of the children being put in the position of getting things wrong all the time can make them become very anti-education. The problem lies in how they learn and how it affects their emotions and then you will see their behaviour – they might do a runner, flip tables, throw chairs and swear. Given strategies, they can become more confident and can ask for help. It may take a year, but it can happen.

I worked in a school for children with severe learning difficulties (SLD) for a year. I remember how on the day I visited the school, a teacher was talking to me and we suddenly heard screeching, swearing and screaming outside the room. In some way I felt as if the teacher was a bit embarrassed by what was happening. She explained that some children in the school have behaviour and communication difficulties that might mean they get upset and violent. I remember saying 'Excellent. That's exactly what I'm looking for, working with children like that'. I loved the work and, coincidentally, worked with that particular child quite often. I learned that building relationships is very important. Having been an outdoor education instructor, I had long hair and I soon found out that this attracted some children to want to touch and pull my hair or spit into it. I had my hair cut and something else I learned was that short hair was an advantage when working with some children who have SLD!

Entering a danger zone

I decided that I wanted to work with pupils in an EBD school. This was the area that interested me most. I took the post as a Year 6 class-room assistant. I had visited the school to help me make my decision. I think that being relaxed and willing to think is very important in working in an EBD school and I hope the pupils see me in this way. I also think that having been to a special school is highly relevant. I have talked to the pupils about it and they know that I can relate to their experiences. I emphasise to them that school can be fun and that you can have a laugh and a joke. I explain that this is very important but that you should also learn when to stop and where the boundaries are as there are times when comments or be-haviour stop being funny. Sometimes their idea of a laugh can go overboard and become disrespectful to other children. I have a system of showing them where the boundaries are. There are two circles, one inside the other. I have explained this system to them. I point to the inside of the inner circle and I explain that this territory is fine and you can have fun there, but if you move out of it then you are entering a danger zone. If you go outside the circle, you are over-stepping the mark – it's not funny any more. I use this by showing them individually what zone they are in, to prevent problems and to help them be aware. I might go to a specific pupil when there is a problem and point to the circle as if to say ' you are in the danger zone and you must try to get back into the circle where things are OK'. I have considered using the circles for the whole group.

There are also ways of dealing with the pupils' concern about fair-ness. We always try to make sure that when there has been a problem involving more than one pupil, we emphasise what everyone has done. We try to resolve the situation fairly so that if they wish to be the best of buddies again, they can do so without anyone feeling hard done by, as this could cause problems.

The status of an LSA

The communication between the teacher and the teaching assistant is very important, as is the communication between school management and teaching assistants. We used to be called classroom assistants but now we are known as teaching assistants. In my school there is a briefing for all staff in the morning and a debriefing at the end of each day. Teaching assistants are invited. The day's events are discussed and so are ideas and strategies. The teachers make sure that the teaching assistants are aware of what is taking place in the lessons and the levels the children are learning at. I may work with two pupils who have similar difficulties and will set up the situation so that they can work together and be supportive of each other. I have the right to work in the way that I want to. There are no real issues about status in my school. There is no low status where teachers look down at teaching assistants. You know that you have high status in my school because you are invited to meetings and you are given the responsibility to solve problems in and out of lessons. Sometimes a teacher will send a pupil to see me to help sort out a problem. This may also be to do with being male in a school where there are more women than men.

I have known situations where supply teachers might see the classroom assistant as a dogsbody. You can be made to feel this way. The teaching assistants work to hold the group together and to keep standards, because they know the children, yet the supply teacher gets so much more money than us. It is not a money issue really, it is a responsibility issue and we have taken most of the responsibility for settling the class and keeping control within the class. There are some good supply teachers but some see you, and treat you, in a very negative way.

Returning to mainstream

For some pupils with EBD, but in my opinion not all, full-time re-integration into mainstream school is possible. Some have been in an EBD school for many years. It is important that integration is talked about and explained to all pupils and those who can be reintegrated or receive integration at some level, such as half a day once a week, feel a massive sense of achievement when it happens. It is brilliant to see their reward for working so hard to get back to mainstream. Part of my role is to support pupils on integration, to help them to succeed, to understand how the mainstream school feels about it and to see whether everyone can cope. This is where there can be an initial problem for the pupil coming from 'an EBD school': the mainstream school might tend to think that there is going to be a behaviour problem. They think this more than thinking there will be a learning problem. They may also see my role as being there to deal with behaviour issues: to sort out problems if they happen. In reality I may be there working with one child from my school but I will have asked the class teacher if there is anyone else I could work with also. No child wants a teaching assistant stuck to their shoulder, it stigmatises them. Also, if you are on integration from an EBD school and someone is stuck to you it looks as if you have brought your own minder along. My preference is to work with anyone in the class who needs help but also to make sure that the pupil from my school is fine. This is what the pupils like and so does the class-teacher.

Befriending
Out of school I am part of a Social Services Befriending scheme. I became involved in this scheme because a boy and his family were talking about it – a type of respite arrangement where someone takes the child out for the afternoon to allow the family to have some time to themselves. The family social worker mentioned the scheme and the boy concerned said he wanted to name a befriender and nominated me. Social Services approached me and I said I would consider this role. I underwent a series of interviews, was accepted for the role and have been working with this one child for two years. Initially there was some anxiety within the school about this arrangement, firstly because it was new and I was one of the first people to be nominated. Then there were issues about the child attending the school and how that affected my role in the school and my relationship with the child. There was some understandable apprehension. After talking with this child, we have together adapted the befriending time so that we sometimes relate what he does in his few hours at the weekend with how well he has met targets at school.

If he has done very well in school he can have real fun during his be-friending time. If he has not done so well we might go for a drive while I talk to him about his work and behaviour at school and how he can improve – as well as talking about other things. There are times when it is important to keep school and home separate and there are times when it is good to link the two. Befriending is a social role whereas being a teaching assistant is an educational role, under-standing the child's learning difficulties and adjusting the work for them.

Seeing changes

Working as a teaching assistant in an EBD school can be very stress-ful. There are times when you feel that the end of the day has been the best part of it. But there are also so many great achievements that you can see. The most enjoyable part of my work is seeing changes take place. Changes for some children are very slow but when any-one reaches a goal that has been set for them everyone is pleased. To see someone fulfil their potential and make progress in reaching a goal that is important for them gives me an excellent feeling. For example I have made certificates for improvement in spellings and to see the children being so happy to receive them is something I like. You see changes like being told that some children cannot hear words so that they can spell them phonetically – perhaps there is a neurological difficulty that prevents them from doing this? Then they work hard and start to sound words out and when you see that happening it gives you a top buzz as a teaching assistant. Then some-one will get one hundred percent for their spellings and that is an unreal feeling for the adults who have helped. For someone like me, who hated school, being part of making these changes happen means that I love school now.

I have seen changes in many pupils but I have also seen changes in myself as a teaching assistant. Having done the job for some time I have begun to think much more about what EBD is: what causes children's difficulties, what prevents their difficulties, what can I, with my experiences and my interests, do to help. The biggest change is that I have become more and more interested in how chil-dren learn. I have learned things myself – practical things like: never to kneel down in front of someone who is very angry as you might get kicked in the face! There are times when children are angry when it helps if the adult backs away from them and their anger. The adult does not always have to watch what the pupil is doing because the pupil might be wanting them to. Also, I have learned how to use emotional times when children are upset to help them to work through their problems. I have learned the benefits of working as part of a team. I have always enjoyed working in teams and this is so important in working with children in special schools.

Redefining EBD

I think that the behaviour part of EBD is emphasised too much. It is often more to do with learning problems. Some people see behaviour first and then they think about education. This means that people can talk about children like this: 'This child's behaviour is unacceptable, they are unteachable. I can't teach them because of their behaviour'. This means the educational difficulties are not looked at. I think that EBD should be labelled in full as *Educational and Behavioural Difficulties*. I know that what children see and what they think and feel has a big effect upon them but I think that their education can set off the behavioural difficulties. When you find learning difficult the educational pressures are big. There are national tests to do where you have to be at a certain level, there is a national curriculum to be learned. In my view, schools should be allowed to adapt what they do to the individuals, go back to square one to where the pupil is, to their level of understanding, and then fewer children would get referred to EBD schools. It might also make more children want to be in school, rather than truant, because they want to learn.

A few months ago I was on a training course for Learning Support Assistants. I was placed in a situation where people were scribing very quickly. Everyone was expected to be able to write at the same quick pace. I could not do it, so I sat back for a minute, I felt emotional. I felt bad about what was happening and had to leave the situation. These were similar feelings to those I would get when I was a child at school. I eventually asked for more time to write, to catch up with everyone else. Children with learning difficulties are worse off than I am because most of them might not be able to do what I did in that situation. They might not have the social skills or the confidence. This is yet another area where a teaching assistant can offer them support.

Points for Reflection and Action

- Spencer draws upon his own experiences as a pupil in special school. What advantages do you see for an LSA in working as an adult in an environment similar to the one where they were once a pupil?

- Managing children's behaviour is often about establishing boundaries. Spencer's story includes many practical suggestions of how this might be done. Talk to a colleague in your school about the merits and pitfalls of his suggestions.

- The 'behaviour' part of EBD, according to Spencer, is what teachers and others think about first of all. He argues that children's difficulties stem from a learning problem. How far do you agree with him?

7

Deborah's Story:
working with Asha

Deborah Skuse

As a teenager I planned to pursue a career as an overseas nanny. This was driven by a combined desire to travel and a love of children but personal circumstances prevented it. Since I am an organised and well-motivated individual, my chosen career was administration-based and I enjoyed working in the computer industry for many years.

My original interest in child development and welfare was restored on the birth of my first daughter. I found that I possessed many qualities well suited to childcare, such as patience and enthusiasm. A natural progression was child-minding, where I had the opportunity to observe children's development, both physical and emotional. In this role I attended short courses organised by the Pre-Playgroup Association and Bristol City Council Social Services Department. This role was, I believe, much respected and I could combine it with my family responsibilities – which I did for four years.

A continued interest in child development led to enrolment on an Access to Teaching course. On completion I obtained a place on a degree course at the University of the West of England, Bristol. Although I successfully competed the first year of a BA (Hons) Literary Studies, for personal reasons I deferred my studies for a year. My direction changed during this year and I enrolled on the

BTEC National Diploma Childhood Studies course. The special educational needs element of the course was interesting and thought-provoking and led to my decision to work in the Early Years field, supporting children with special needs. As a Learning Support Assistant I believe I have many of the attributes needed for the job: flexibility and adaptability, a calm manner, good communication skills, energy, being understanding, and a sense of humour.

All about Asha

Since September 2000 I have been working part-time (25 hours a week) in a Reception class at a multicultural inner city primary school. The child I am mainly working with has a statement for a variety of special needs, including visual impairment and global developmental delay. She has siblings at the school and comes from a supportive home environment in which Somali is the home language. In order to maintain confidentiality I shall call her Asha.

Until recently Asha received a block course of physiotherapy as she has poor upper body movement and has difficulties with fine motor skills. She has a cheery disposition and good social skills; she is a popular member of the class. Asha and I work alongside a group of five other children, four of whom have English as an additional language (EAL); their home language is Urdu. Our last group member is the youngest in the class and understandably immature; this manifests itself in a general lack of understanding in lessons and subsequent disruptive behaviour. The home environment of the other four in the group is less supportive than Asha's, and all have developmental and behavioural difficulties and are currently on Stage Two of the Code of Practice. The class teacher feels that these children will all benefit from working together with me. But Asha's progress is my priority, in line with the content of her statement of SEN.

I support this group during both the literacy and numeracy strategies, working within the structure of the Foundation Stage of the National Curriculum. I aim to keep the children on task during whole-class teaching and to support the class teacher, using a number of different materials and resources suited to the individual. During small-group time I carry on the work previously introduced, where my focus is on each child: this allows them individual time to reinforce their understanding and knowledge. The majority of the group are making good academic progress and are also developing their social skills.

All in a day's work

Introducing and maintaining clear expectations for children has been a personal success for me. Clear expectations of behaviour have been agreed between myself and each child. I believe this is vital to the security and success of the group. Generally the children are relaxed, settled and, with encouragement from me, they remain on task. Pastoral care is important, I believe, as it underpins the child's overall well-being and helps in developing high levels of self-esteem and positive self-image. I use a number of different strategies to encourage and develop the children's understanding, such as praise, modelling, positive reinforcement and humour. Many of the children display poor self-image; believing themselves to be 'worthless' and 'naughty'. Their confidence is low and independence needs to be continuously encouraged. Children need appropriate stimulation and opportunities to be risk-takers in a safe and secure environment. I praise each individual child, allowing them to work within their own potential.

Good social skills are vital to social acceptance and inclusion. With the additional support that I am able to provide, the children appear to be less disruptive to the rest of the class. More importantly, they are making steady progress in terms of developing their social skills. I encourage the group to be vocal and ensure that I am an attentive listener. However, whilst I am pleased with class behaviour, play-times are generally difficult. Perhaps a more structured break would give then the security to develop a sense of play and be risk-takers without displaying aggressive behaviour?

My ICT skills have been well utilised by the class teacher in planning weekly sessions in the newly installed ICT suite. Here I work in mixed ability groups of up to twelve children working with various early years programmes. This gives me the opportunity to build relationships with the entire class. The children are relaxed in my company and do not hesitate to ask for assistance. Equally, I have a good grasp of their individual needs and am able to support them whenever necessary. The majority of the children enjoy ICT and work well, since it requires different skills from working with print. Asha uses a mouse which is smaller than normal, allowing her to hold it more comfortably. With the mouse in place she is able to be more independent and operates cause and effect programmes with ease. Her improving self-image is almost visible.

Working within the Foundation Stage should ensure that all children in a Reception class have the right to learn through play. Resources should be available to support this initiative, from outdoor play equipment such as bicycles to imaginative role-play. Again, as an LSA I am integrally involved in these activities. Inevitably, inadequate funding is frustrating for all members of the school community.

The role of the learning support assistant is multi-faceted. In addition to working with the children I also support the class teacher and school by performing many other tasks, from planning and organising imaginative wall displays to creating and maintaining resources and materials. One of my personal concerns is the lack of opportunity for the child to express him/herself within the school day. The constraints of the timetable do not allow for listening to the voice of the child. The child's voice is less dominant than those of the adults around him/her and there is consequently a tendency for this voice to be lost.

A good working relationship is vital to a successful class and school team. I am a valued team member and my contributions and experience are much appreciated. My knowledge and understanding of ICT is highly valued by the class teacher and is put to good use. Time constraints are not conducive to effective planning or to monitoring and assessment. In common with many LSAs, this usually has to be done *en route* to the staffroom! Planning time is not built into my daily programme and is often *ad hoc*. The telephone helps me to complete many of these tasks after hours.

The wider context

LSAs, or teaching assistants, play a valuable role in school. The Government appears to be working at raising standards in this field, and I fully support this. Outside agencies and professionals should have a clear understanding of the importance of the role of the LSA. Working part-time means that I am not available at the beginning and end of the school day. Any concerns raised at those times would be referred to the class teacher who is held responsible by the school and manages any daily issues. However, Asha's review meetings are held each half term and give the opportunity for a number of outside agencies such as occupational therapists and the visual impairment specialist teacher to plan and discuss targets with the class teacher, her mother and myself.

Bristol City Council runs a comprehensive training programme for LSAs, for which schools incur costs for their involvement. Lack of supply cover for LSAs can militate against the take-up of such training opportunities. I have recently attended a government-sponsored pilot scheme of induction training for teacher assistants (TA). This course stressed the importance of the TA, and included inputs on behaviour management, literacy and numeracy and special educational needs. Specific to my current role, I attended a two day Visual Impairment course in order to acquire a better understanding of Asha's visual needs. Out of personal interest, I will be joining a one-day Counselling for Children workshop held by University of Bristol, aimed at children aged seven to eleven and hope that it will help me decide my career path when planning my future.

At present I find my current role fulfilling and I intend to remain with Asha throughout Key Stage One. But I would like the option to review plans within the next three years. Ideally I would prefer to obtain credits through the continuing professional development (CPD) initiative at the University since this suits my family commitments. Obtaining degree status in this manner would enable me to consider training as a teacher in the future.

I am also considering returning to my Literary Studies degree on a part-time basis. Another possibility is to pursue my interest in counselling skills for children. I enjoy working with young children and see my future in this field. It is a rewarding experience, which requires a great many skills. I would recommend the job of LSA to anyone considering working with children. Perhaps new Government initiatives will include raising the profile and status of LSAs as well as providing more appropriate financial remuneration.

Points for Reflection and Action

• Deborah talks about the need to establish a good working relationship between LSA and teacher. How would you define this, from the perspective of an LSA?

• Training and professional development are crucial to the development of an LSA. Deborah's story hints at some of the obstacles to LSAs in accessing some of the opportunities available to them. From your own experience can you add others? Conversely, do recent initiatives in professional development for LSAs present a more optimistic picture?

• As part of her work Deborah is involved in providing additional support to some children during literacy and numeracy sessions. How do you think an LSA might support a class teacher most effectively during these sessions?

8

Janet's story: working with Georghie

Janet Martin

I am married and have three children, the youngest of whom is sixteen. I received what I describe as a 'moderate' education at school, and left with only a few formal qualifications. I attended school at a time when only 'bright' pupils seemed to get pushed and expectations for girls in particular were at lot lower than they are today. I could have achieved better grades but at the time I was only interested in getting a job to earn some money before I got married and had children. I had my children at an early age and I feel that this factor has provided me with many of the qualities necessary to be a successful learning support assistant. Working at primary school level, a learning support assistant needs to have:

- a good sense of humour

- common sense

- empathy with, and understanding of, children

- the ability to get on with other people

These qualities are learnt through life skills rather than formal qualifications. All my previous jobs have involved working face-to-face with the general public, especially the elderly. As my own children got older I felt that I would like to pursue a career with children. I contacted my local college and found out about a course that would enable me to work towards a recognised qualification in working with children. This course required me to work every afternoon in my local infants school, which I did voluntarily. As I was also work-ing part-time it was sometimes quite difficult to juggle my time to cover the three things together. In fact, had I not enjoyed my time in school so much it would have been very easy to throw in the towel.

I worked voluntarily in school for two years and then was offered a job working on a part-time basis with a child with cerebral palsy, who attended the same school. When this child transferred to junior school she progressed to full integration in mainstream education and I was employed to work with her for twenty hours a week. Georghie is now ten years old and because of being kept back a year she is in Year Five. She is both physically and visually impaired and has significant learning disabilities, all caused by the cerebral palsy. She is unable to travel around the school independently and needs a lot of help to access the National Curriculum successfully. Georghie is on Stage Five of the Code of Practice and is on the school's special needs register. As well as the help she receives from me, she has regular visits from her physiotherapist, a member of the peripatetic team for the visually impaired and she attends two half-hour lessons from the school's special needs teacher, along with other children from the class.

As Georghie's learning support assistant it is my job to support her by:

- helping her to cope with the everyday pressures of the classroom

- helping her to understand what the class teacher is saying by ex-plaining in an alternative or more simplistic manner if appro-priate.

- physically enlarging written materials to enable her to access curriculum materials

- assisting her with her physical and personal needs whilst at the same trying to encourage her independence.

My main aim in doing this is to encourage Georghie to learn at her own pace, to encourage and help her work without doing the work for her and not to let her become over-dependent upon me.

Although Georghie has a lot of problems she is a happy, well-adjusted child. She is the middle child in the family and has not been allowed to dwell on her disabilities. She has a good go at everything and accepts that some things are beyond her capabilities. She sometimes needs to be encouraged to give new experiences a try rather than assuming that she won't be able to do them. She also sometimes needs to be reminded that she is a member of the class rather than 'special': for instance if the class is kept in for bad behaviour that also includes her!

Working with Georghie is very rewarding but it can also be frustrating. Breakthroughs achieved one day are seemingly forgotten the next. Her learning ability is very dependent upon how she is feeling and even on the time of day. She is likely to switch off if she doesn't like a particular lesson and needs to be brought back on task. She is not confident enough to answer questions in a whole-class situation unless she runs the answer by me first. I encourage her to have a go even if the answer she supplies is incorrect. Georghie responds well to a lot of praise whilst at the same time expecting praise for every small task she does. I tend to give her small stickers if she has worked really well – but not too often, as she is inclined to expect them for everything.

My work with Georghie means that I am mainly based in one classroom. Because of her needs I sit by her for much of the time but the other children know that I am available for them as well, particularly the group of children in the class who have particular difficulties with their learning. Georghie often resents the fact that I work with other children and will persistently tap me on the arm to ask me to look at her work. I have tried to get around this problem by telling her that she must wait if I am talking to another child and that if she needs me she must put up her hand in the same way as the other children rather than calling out my name. As well as working with Georghie I also teach the additional literacy support group, which is quite enjoyable and I work with Year 3 children for two hours a week.

On reflection, there are things that really concern me about the work that I do. These are:

- the fact that my job is dependent upon one child's attendance at school. I do worry about what I will do when Georghie goes to secondary school.

- how Georghie will manage at secondary school, especially if she attends a unit at a mainstream school where she may not have her own learning support assistant.

Points for Reflection and action

- In Janet's story she recounts her individual work with Georghie. She deals effectively with the successes and frustrations of such a relationship. What strategies do you think an LSA needs to help them deal with such close attachment to a single pupil?

- Janet describes how sometimes she works with other groups of children in Georghie's class – sometimes much to the resentment of Georghie herself. What dilemmas are there for an LSA in determining who, when, and at what level, additional support is needed in the classroom?

- How might the 'job insecurity' Janet refers to in her conclusion best be overcome?

9

Joanne and Michele's story: working with John

Joanne Robinson and Michele Burgess

Selective Mutism is a term used for children who talk freely in some situations but are silent in others. The pupil we were asked to support spoke to family members at home but to no one outside. In this chapter he is called John. John was to receive full-time support when he started in secondary school in September 1999. As learning support workers (LSW) we were to provide this support, and were to do this as a job-share position between us.

We both now support John in his new school, a mainstream 11-16 secondary school, where we are attached to the Learning Support Department. The Department currently has around 20 LSAs and we all help to support pupils with a wide range of special educational needs across the curriculum, from Year 7 to Year 11. We are officially employed by Gloucester Special Educational Needs Area Resource Centre (SENARC).

On arrival at the school we were given guidelines on supporting the pupil and an indication of those areas which could potentially be difficult for any pupil starting secondary school. When we met John in the first week of term, he appeared to be very self-conscious and would not give us any eye contact at first. He behaved well and was very organised although he seemed to have some obsessive habits with his pencil-case and books. He was also reluctant to let you see his work and was quite secretive. Eventually we were able to gain his trust and he started to make both sounds and eye contact.

Selecting and adapting a programme for Selective Mutism

Through our special educational needs co-ordinator (SENCO) and other colleagues, we heard of a programme called *Breaking Down the Barriers*, developed by Maggie Johnson and Anthony H. Glassberg. One of the difficulties we encountered was that very little appeared to be known about children with Selective Mutism and we believe that John was the only such pupil in the County. We felt that one of our chief aims was to give John the opportunity to speak in school: this programme seemed the most suitable.

After a meeting with our SENCO and head of the SEN support service, we agreed that it would be a good idea to try and begin the programme at the end of March. We felt that by that time we would have built up a sufficiently good rapport with John and gained his trust. Firstly, though, we had to find a suitable *private* room in the school and order some resources, as the first stage of the programme revolved around a series of games and activities without speech.

The programme duly started near the end of March. We had some initial difficulty in finding time in the pupil's timetable to do our work, as it was important he was not withdrawn from lessons for just ten minutes, thereby creating all sorts of disruption. So, with John's and his parents' agreement, we took ten minutes during the lunch hour and booked the nurses' room, a small private room, on a daily basis.

John enjoyed the activities, which involved a variety of puzzles, games and mime. He was very self-conscious at first but soon became involved in the activities. We achieved the initial target of making John feel relaxed and comfortable with us quite quickly. We then moved on to the next stage, where he had to give gestures to indicate what he meant. We played games which incorporated this task. As he already made gestures in the classroom and could communicate quite well without speech, we started by using this.

First Sounds

After Easter that year we resumed this work, partly to remind him of what we had been doing before the holidays. He quickly passed through this revision stage and arrived at that part of the programme which we thought would prove the most testing for him: John was to make sounds! He had made a few sounds in the classroom and, sometimes when he was frustrated or excited, had made a sound which definitely resembled a word or phrase. Once he realised he had done this he became very guarded. This stage was very difficult for him at first and he initially refused to make any sounds at all. He was extremely self-conscious and seemed uncomfortable at times. He had many delaying tactics but usually he would eventually take part in the activities we had planned for the programme. Over time John gradually began to participate, sometimes when one of us was out of the room or looking at the wall. This was the most difficult part of the structured intervention plan; it required patience and continual reinforcement.

By this stage we had started an achievement sticker sheet. This was recommended by the programme's authors: when John reached a given target he was allowed to choose a sticker for his sheet. This proved quite successful and he enjoyed having the chance to make a choice. It was clear that he wanted to progress and liked to be rewarded and praised when a target had been met.

By the end of June he was happy to say sounds and to give eye contact as he did so. He started recording into a small hand-held tape recorder from home. During July he even started to say the odd word but used avoidance strategies, like hiding under the table or waiting until we were out of the room. It was soon the end of the summer term and the holiday period would be a long break. This could be a point at which John's progress in the programme came under threat. After quite a lot of thought we decided that the most reasonable thing we could request him to do was to keep a diary on tape, throughout the holiday period.

A breakthrough...

The autumn term started with the programme slowly being reintroduced. Our main fear at this stage was that all the work we had previously done would be lost because it had not been reinforced during holiday time. But we were proved wrong: John was still happy to continue with the programme and started reading words from a book and from work sheets. This began to develop into reading sentences and we practised telephone conversations, even ringing him at home. He was far more comfortable talking now and was happy to read plays sitting on a chair and having conversations about different social situations.

Though we considered this to be a great achievement on his part we also believed that it was time to move on. It was now mid-November and we had to introduce other people into the room. He was now speaking freely during sessions with the LSWs, so we felt we could challenge him further.

Introducing speech with peers and teachers

At lunch-time we brought in four pupils from John's form group and he reluctantly spoke to them behind one of the cabinets in the room. Gradually this situation improved, and as we played word games with up to four or five pupils, he gained confidence enough to make eye contact and speak. His major breakthrough at this stage was speaking his German aural on tape and having the work marked.

After the Christmas break, John was set the target of saying 'Yes' when his form tutor called out his name during registration. We first of all spoke to his form tutor and agreed how to go about this. John would be given until half-term to succeed. This would still be difficult for him, as registration takes place in his form room and in front of the class. So we began by gradually introducing sessions in the form room with a limited number of pupils present. John was able to meet this target by half-term and still continues to answer to the register now.

John has since spoken to our SENCO during English workshop lessons, as well as to a number of other teachers. We are still continuing with the programme and his new targets are to speak to his LSW in lessons and to try to restrict his use of gesture, which has built up over the years when he chose not to speak.

What about the future?

We will both continue with John's programme and hope he will further overcome his anxiety so that when he needs to speak to teachers and his peers he feels he can do so. He continues to make progress and has started to speak in lessons – albeit very quietly and in short sentences. We could not have imagined this a year ago when we began the programme. At present most speech is directed to his LSWs and he is very conscious of his peers listening.

We have learnt a great deal about Selective Mutism in our work with John. It appears that there are a number of factors, which prevent such children and young people from speaking:

- **anxiety** – some children worry about not knowing what to say during a discussion or in response to a teacher's question. Children will not take a risk for fear of being wrong: they prefer to stay silent.

- **direct questioning** – this puts the child on the spot; it can cause them both panic and embarrassment. They do not seem to like this kind of attention and often appear to be very shy.

- **structured speech** – it is difficult for children to answer a question if they have not rehearsed their answer beforehand. We both spent a great deal of time during the programme writing conversations and different scenes, so that John might be able to use them to make him feel more comfortable in social situations.

- **surroundings** – the rooms we used for the programme were always the same in the initial stages of our intervention: the nurses' room and Head of Year's room. These were both small and very private. Eventually we would walk around the whole school building, playing games and other activities. During this time we moved to larger rooms where there was not the same sense of security for John because teachers and other pupils could walk in unannounced.

All these factors contribute to a child not wanting to speak and to a build-up of a fear of speech, resulting in their unwillingness to verbalise. We discovered that selective mutism is a complex condition, which has to be dealt with sensitively and slowly. Building up trust

with the pupil is the basis on which he or she can begin the slow process of communicating verbally with others.

Points for Reflection and Action

- The school in which Michele and Joanne work employs about 20 LSAs. What are the possible advantages and opportunities to be derived from this 'critical mass'?

- Michele and Joanne describe how they have found and imple-mented an individual programme to support John. How can the process they describe be valuable in assisting LSAs to develop and evaluate individual interventions?

- In their story Michele and Joanne identify what they have learnt about selective mutism. Can you see any connections between their findings and their relevance to working with children with other special educational needs?

10

Carole's story: looking back

Carole Rose

I was an LSA in a special school for eighteen years. I first became a welfare assistant in an all-age special school for what were then known as maladjusted children. That is how the children were classed: they were 'maladjusted children' and were all grouped together. It was years later that the term changed to 'children with behavioural difficulties' and later still to 'children with emotional and behavioural difficulties' (EBD). The school had no links with other schools or with the local community. The children were not always in school, going out regularly on trips and outdoor activities – but there were some difficulties. I remember an occasion when some older boys went to an amusement park and climbed on to the highest roof in the park. It was very dangerous. It was thought that taking the children out of the school would be helpful to them but that was not always the case.

The children would often say that they were not normal because of the school they attended and because of the labels used to describe them. There were times when the children would behave in a way that was unacceptable and use a label to explain what they were doing, almost as if it gave them an excuse. They would say 'well, what do you expect? I am in a school for children with behavioural difficulties'. They would talk about mainstream school as 'normal school' and were very negative about attending a special school. Some had been excluded from the mainstream and so they saw their new school as not being for 'normal' children. One of the biggest and most difficult challenges for anyone who works with children like that is to change the childrens' view of themselves and who they are; to change the view that they are not normal because they go to a special school.

Becoming a Welfare Assistant

I knew when I had my own children that I did not want to stay working in an office and wanted the rest of my working life to be spent with children. Before I became a welfare assistant I ran a playgroup for children aged three to five who were not able to remain in other playgroups because of their behaviour. Some would also attend as a part of a hospital referral. I would get told that these were children that nobody else could handle and I liked working with them. I enjoyed being with children who had different kinds of difficulties. This may well be because I was quite naughty when I was at school – I talked too much, I liked to make other children laugh and would get into trouble for doing things like throwing my pastry onto the ceiling during a cooking lesson because I thought it was funny. I enjoyed a bit of mischief and was on very good terms with the door to the headmaster's office.

Early days

My first day as an assistant was one of horror. Schools were not as organised as they are now; there was no national curriculum, for example. The class of five and six year olds I was going to work with had been having lots of different teachers and the day I began there was no teacher for them at all! A senior teacher in the school sent me to the classroom and simply left me there. I was in a room with six boys and one girl whom I knew nothing about and there was no teacher in there with me. The children did not know me, they had never seen me before, and they must have thought they were in for a great time with a new person. They promptly opened the doors to the playground and all ran away. The doors had been locked but they knew how to open them. I didn't know what to do. I did know that if I chased them I would not be able to catch them. Some were in the playground, others had run into a large field. I told them to come back and they started making abusive signs and swearing at me.

There I was, a complete novice, left to deal with this on my own. Instead of carrying on telling them what to do and being ignored or sworn at, I thought about what was happening and realised that what I was doing was not working at all. So I made a conscious decision to go back into the classroom, where I sat down and began reading a book. I could see the children and noticed they were beginning to realise that there was not going to be a chase. After a while they slowly started to come back in. I sat there and waited for them to return. They were completely unaware that my stomach was churning all the time because I didn't know if I was doing the right thing or if it would work. I learnt many lessons from this first experience. I learned that to do the job of an LSA in an EBD school you have to try lots of different tactics. You have think quickly and make quick decisions.

I remember another incident that took place early on in my career. I was on duty in the playground and I had heard rumours that there was trouble brewing between two of the oldest pupils, a boy and a girl. It was a grim day and I was on playground duty on my own. I had heard that the girl was going to 'mark' the boy – a phrase used by the children to describe someone being knifed. Being on my own left me in a potentially vulnerable situation. I suddenly sensed that there was trouble in the air – to this day I don't know how, it is just something that you do. I looked and saw the girl rushing towards the boy. I stepped in between the two of them to stop the problem. The girl was reaching around me and grabbing the boy's hair and then I saw a knife. I held her hand against a fence because this was the hand with the knife in it. There was nobody around to help me and as you can imagine, the children all gathered to watch what was happening. To me it felt as if the children were thinking 'Wow, this is a brilliant bit of lunchtime entertainment'. I was really panicking inside, as I didn't know how long I could hold on to her and felt that either me or the boy was going to get cut. I calmly asked her to let go of the knife but she would not. I had to look at the children who were watching and pick one I could trust – and who I knew the staff would believe – and demand that he get help straight away. He ran inside and a teacher came out and the problem was sorted.

I made sure that I talked to the girl about what she had done so that she realised how serious I thought it was. In those days I always felt that talking was very important and I continue to believe this throughout my time working with children with EBD. When there is an incident, they need to talk about what happened and to be listened to as well. You can be very firm when creating boundaries but this works better when the children feel that they are listened to. They need to talk about why they are at the school too, not in a way that makes them feel abnormal but in a way that helps them deal with any problems they have, to get support.

Early images

My memory of my early years as a welfare assistant includes images of time spent chasing children around the school grounds. The children would run off and we would have to find them, while the teacher carried on working with the group. To be honest, there were some aspects of work in the early 1980s that I was very unhappy about. One was the fact that the adults in the school used to wander around as if they worked in a jail. I remember having to carry bunches of keys and being told that I had constantly to lock doors – this was done to keep the children in or keep them out. Children would walk down corridors and after we opened a door to move along, we would lock it behind us. I think this was bad practice but at the time it was seen as the norm and everyone did it. Another practice you would see was children being held down and restrained when they were behaving badly. This was not the norm, not everyone did it, but for some people it was what they did first, rather that trying to find another way of solving a problem. Children experiencing EBD do get violent and there are times when, for safety reasons, they may need to be restrained. I have always felt that holding children down or using force should never be the first thing you try.

Good practice in the classroom

My first impression when I came into a classroom for children who were at a school for the maladjusted was 'yuk!' The classrooms were awful places; it was hard to find anything at all that was pleasant about them. When you talked to some people about improving the classroom environment, you would be told that you could not put work on the walls because the children would rip it down and destroy it. You were told not to put plants in the room because although you thought it would make the room look better, the children would damage the plants or smash the pots. Whatever you suggested you were told that these children would do their best to ruin the efforts you made because they were disturbed. Similar arguments have been put forward during my years as an LSA. It was not until I worked with a teacher who did not share this view that I had a chance to try it out and see what would happen: if we made the environment look good, would the children destroy it?

The teacher said she wanted the classroom to look like a place where children were learning. I told her that I felt the school looked more like a unit than a school. She was brilliant at her job and it became clear to me that the personality, skills and attitude of the teacher is one of the most important elements of making an EBD school successful. She respected my views and we worked as a team. We felt differently from the majority of the teachers who had an idea that the children would wreck the environment. We believed that the environment said a lot about how we viewed the children and we decided that if we made a big effort to make it look nice, then they would treat it well and feel good about themselves. We set about the task of making the room look pleasant and exciting. We put work on the walls but soon found out that the others were right – the children ripped it down! What we did was to put it back up again, but then as soon as we had done that they ripped it down again. We then decided to talk to them and explain that ripping the work down was in a way hurting themselves because it was saying that their efforts were not valuable. It did not hurt us, we did not like it if they tore the work down but it did not say anything about us – we would just put it back up time after time because we believed they were worth it. I remember saying that they had to know that we wanted the room to look good, to show what they can do, to show things to be proud of, and that we wanted to work in a room like that too. To put displays of children's work on the walls may seem commonplace now, as would making great efforts to make the rooms look pleasant, but then it was not the done thing – one reason being that the children did not do much work.

Support and the curriculum

It may seem strange nowadays, but the teachers decided what the children should do in their lessons. There was no plan coming down from the government or the headteacher. I began as an assistant working with younger children. You could work with one teacher who thought that the children had to play for most of the time. Then you would meet another who wanted the children to work from worksheets. Sometime you would meet a teacher who wanted some maths done in a book; others didn't mind if it was done without a book. Some teachers thought that too much work would cause the children to flip: to become cross and angry and cause trouble. Other teachers thought too much play would have this effect. It must have been difficult for the children because with one teacher they sat at desks most of the time, with another they played most of the time. There was maths and English and, as I remember, every afternoon was for play.

The curriculum was influenced by the views of the teachers. The way to help the children was also dependent upon the teachers' views. You could have people working in all sorts of different ways in the same school. Some tried to change the behaviour of the children by talking to them but others thought that behaving in certain ways allowed children to get their problems out of their system. There was no set curriculum until the national curriculum was introduced. There was not much planning but there were some teachers who would plan and talk to you about what they were intending to do. It is important to realise that it is the teacher who is responsible and accountable for what is in the curriculum and how it should be taught. My job was to support the learning of the children and this is why assistants need to communicate with the teacher about what is planned.

The only time I felt responsible for teaching the class was when there was a supply teacher who seemed to have no control at all and the LSA had to take over. As an LSA, you know nothing about supply teachers and what training they have. You don't know if you will get someone who is very good or someone who will go into the stockroom and lock themselves in to get away from the children –

which I saw happen once. Even today, LSAs can have a difficult time when there are supply teachers. It can happen when the supply teacher is not even in your classroom but you hear what is happening in a nearby room; you feel responsible for helping the children and want to go and help.

Being an LSA in a 'failing school'

The school I worked in for many years was then inspected by government inspectors and we were told that the school was failing. LSAs had an opportunity to talk to the inspectors when we were all organised into discussion groups, but it is very difficult to speak your mind in such a group because you are sitting with colleagues, some of whom are friends, and you have to be careful about saying anything that could be seen to be negative about what you see each day and what you know to be wrong. You know who you think is doing a good job and who is not. Working with different teachers, you pick this up very quickly. The inspectors have to see it for themselves as I am not sure that, at that time, support assistants would have been taken as seriously as they might be now.

There was a time when if you expressed a view about how the children learn or what they were learning some teachers might think, 'what do you know – you are only a welfare assistant'. It was as if it wasn't part of your job to comment on what happened in the classroom. You cannot work as a team if some people will not let others have responsibilities or ideas on how to help. In my experience, if you feel good about how you work with the children, they can tell, so it is important that everyone feels good and shares ideas. The inspectors are important, but the real judges should be the children.

It was ten years ago that the inspectors said that the school I worked in was failing. I can remember how many people were threatened by what they said. For support assistants one of the main worries was that the school would be closed down and you would lose your job. That is hard for anyone who knows they could not be doing their job any better than they were at the time of the inspection. The communication between teaching staff and support staff could probably have been better, although in some teams it was excellent. As a support assistant you were aware of the tensions in the school about what was going on.

Finally, a new headteacher was appointed. He talked about the national curriculum which some people found threatening. Some staff said openly that, because of the nature of the children, they could not run the school like a mainstream school. I was working part-time. I found myself becoming unhappy over the fact that although I was doing my best, as were many others, there were difficulties I could do nothing about as a support assistant. I was not in a position to make big changes. A strong headteacher and senior teachers were needed to show a direction for the school. By strong leadership in action, I mean people who are willing to listen to others and accept their views but also have a clear view of where the school is going and a good knowledge of the children. My school now had strong leadership and this had a big effect on how I felt about my job.

There was a new approach towards communication between staff so that everyone was involved. There was also a new sense of trust – this is really important for support assistants as it shows them respect. If you are not doing things as the people who are responsible for running the school would want you to, you have then no problem with them showing you a new and a better way of doing your work if you know they trust you. There are also times where you see practice that you feel is unacceptable and it is important to speak to someone about it. Not that I would feel comfortable talking about something relating to how a teacher is teaching the curriculum or about school-based developments. I mean situations where you are concerned about the safety of the children, including their emotional safety, for example: physical restraint, racist abuse, threatening behaviour. You have to feel that you are in a position where you can speak up and that being a support assistant makes no difference when discussing things that concern you.

You also have to be aware that there are times when a support assistant might have problems working with a teacher and vice versa, and schools have to support both people when this happens. I advise anyone in this situation to speak to a member of the senior management about it so that problems can be sorted out, otherwise the children do not learn about relationships. They do not see two people showing them how to get on together. There could be many reasons for this – personalities could be one. Experience may be another – a new teacher might come to work with a class where the assistant has known the children for years. This calls for a lot of thinking about how to develop a working relationship. In a teacher/ LSA relationship, nobody should try to put the other person in their place. One should not be threatened by the other; they should value each other's experience. It has to be accepted that in a classroom where there is more than one adult, some children will choose who they speak to if they are sad or angry.

And it changes: there are times when a child will choose to speak with the assistant but a few weeks later they may turn to the teacher. I have never wanted to be a teacher; I didn't become an LSA because secretly I want to be a teacher. I think there are differences between being a teacher and being an assistant and those differences should be recognised. As an assistant who worked for eighteen years in an EBD school, I have seen many teachers and have observed how brilliant some of them have been at their job.

Good teachers I have seen

You can spot a teacher who will be good at working with children with EBD almost as soon as they enter the classroom. They have a personality that comes across immediately. They have a calm approach and manner but they also have a real air of authority about them – not an authority that comes across as if they are looking to challenge the children but a way of behaving as if they are in charge of what is happening and making sure that things are OK. Good teachers I have worked with seldom shout and try hard to provide interesting lessons. Their teaching is varied, what the children do is varied and keeps their attention. In EBD schools children can get very upset and angry and I have seen some teachers use clever ways of getting the children back to doing their work. The also have a calm way of getting the other children out of the class if there is a serious problem with a child that has flipped. They know what will make the situation better and they might stay in the room themselves or they might ask the assistant to stay. I have been in situations where

I have been showered with pencils, chairs and everything else available to throw. But I know that I am there because the teacher feels that I am the best person to put up with the bombardment so that, in the end, it can be sorted out for the child. I might be very frightened inside but I would never show it.

LSAs need to work in exactly the same calm way as a good teacher. You can learn so much from a good teacher. This is how working as a team begins: knowing you can depend on each other to be calm, especially when things become difficult. It shows the children that a calm approach can help to solve problems. It is also important that the teacher/assistant relationship is based upon mutual trust.

Learning from experience

From my experience, I have found that key things are important when supporting children who have learning and behavioural problems. Most importantly you have to like children, accepting them and their difficulties. You should also:

- Keep your sense of humour. It is good for the children to be able to join in laughter together and with the adults

- Find what is likeable about the children and tell them about it

- Be patient and work hard at being patient

- Be calm. If you are in a difficult situation, learn how to appear calm – even if you feel worried inside

- Be prepared to see and hear things that might be shocking but do not be shocked by them

- Remember that when children get angry they will eventually calm down again

- Help children to look at a problem by talking about what went wrong, where it went wrong and how it could be avoided in the future

- Never bear a grudge against a child. Children may be verbally or physically abusive – they might give out a lot towards you – but you must give back ways of making relationships work

- Do not take abuse personally

- Learn by your mistakes – everybody makes mistakes

- Always be alert and aware of actions and reactions in the classroom. Do not necessarily show the children by your behaviour that you are alert , otherwise they may feel that every move they make is being watched (even though it might be!). Being alert allows you to diffuse potential difficulties

- Do not pry into the lives of children but be aware of the reasons why they are in a special and not a mainstream school. It could be for many reasons, such as physical or sexual abuse, home life difficulties, a desperate need for individual time and attention and in some cases medical or brain problems

- Some children will have had more tellings off and beatings than you could imagine before they come to an EBD school. The adults who work with them in the school have to find another way – a different way. Most children will eventually respond to kindness. A special school should be like time out from all the things that have not worked before in the mainstream, so that the children can receive individual help with their problems. If the time out works well, then some children can return to mainstream school

- Be proud of your achievements, as you can make a big difference to someone's life. In many years time someone, somewhere who you supported years ago might look back at their time in school and say... *'I remember that LSA. She respected me and was kind to me when I was feeling horrible. No matter what I did, she always found time for a kind word – she made a difference to how I felt about myself then and how I feel about myself now'*.

Points for Reflection and Action

- Since Carole started working in a special school, the terminology relating to children perceived as experiencing 'emotional and/or behavioural difficulties' has changed, To what degree do you think that the role of the LSA itself has also changed?

- Examine Carole's list of what she has learnt from her experience as an LSA. Which of the attributes that she mentions do you see as being the most important? Why? (Try to restrict your selection to just three!)

- What does Carole see as the positives and negatives of LSAs and teachers working together in supporting children who experience behaviour difficulties? To what extent can any resulting professional tensions be resolved?

11

Lin's story: the highs and lows of a teaching assistant

Lin Dyer

Wanted: One caring, flexible, versatile, intelligent, listening, advice-giving, behaviour-managing, moral-boosting, negotiating, consistent, team-playing individual (who can also make a mean cup of tea!)

This could be an advertisement for today's teaching assistant. A little exaggerated, I know, but for all that it includes many of the qualities that teaching assistants are expected to bring to the job. So how come I find myself, at the age of 50, presuming to be this paragon of virtue: a learning support assistant?

I suppose, when I look back, I should have entered the teaching profession on leaving school. I always enjoyed my school life, both at primary and grammar school. But I left after taking and passing 8 GCSE '0' levels and entered the Civil Service, a job I also greatly enjoyed. In time, I married and had my own children and always took an interest in their education, becoming involved whenever I could. Luckily for me, my children's schools always welcomed parental involvement and I found I was greatly enjoying my taste of school life from the 'other side'. So when the head of my son's junior school told me that a general assistant's job for 6 hours a week was coming up, I was only too pleased to apply. And so began my life as a general assistant.

I have been doing the job in various guises (general assistant, learning support assistant, teaching assistant and, latterly, specialist teaching assistant) for over 14 years now so I must get something out of it! Primarily I enjoy working with seven to eleven year olds. By this time they have settled into school life and their personalities shine through. I see them go from slightly worried seven year olds about to enter 'big' school to eleven year olds, well equipped for the life at senior school. I like to think that this is due, in some small way, to the support and encouragement I have been able to give them. A simple hug or 'Thanks Miss, I enjoyed that' at the end of a science investigation can speak volumes and makes up for all those head banging times that leave me frustrated. The teaching staff seems to appreciate and respect me, feelings which are mutual. I feel valued as a member of the school team.

Being flexible

As specialist teaching assistant, I work with children of all abilities and aptitudes across Years 3 to 6. I greatly enjoy science and art and am also the school governor with a special interest in numeracy. However, I assist in all subject areas across the curriculum (except music) and also in the preparation of materials and teaching aids. I find flexibility a distinct advantage. Although I do have a timetable to work to, things can happen in such a way that I could find myself working in a different class and with a different child to the one I was expecting.

Thinking on the move is one of the things I really like about the job. No two days are ever the same, children being children, and I feel this keeps me on the ball. I love the feeling of being involved in all aspects of school life from actual instruction and support through to helping with discipline. I feel that we (the school) are an extended family for the child, being there not just for the academic things. I hope I always take an interest in each child and their likes and dislikes and feel on the whole that they give me their respect.

However, I feel I don't always succeed with all the children. They are all individuals with their own personalities and, just as we don't get on with all adults in life, so I don't always find it easy to get through to certain children. I find talking things over with other adults in school – teachers and other teaching assistants – can help, especially as a different approach to a problem is often suggested. I feel, though, that you should never give up on the children who are particularly difficult. As one boy said to me recently, after I had reminded him, yet again, that his behaviour was not acceptable, 'You never give up Miss!'. My answer was 'No, and I never will'.

My working week is made up of lots of little successes. As an example, I can describe one strategy used recently that that worked for me: it involved the use of a stopwatch and some photos. A Year 4 boy had been having trouble concentrating and sitting still. He constantly demanded attention and the class teacher was beginning to despair of him. Our headteacher increased my hours in this particular class so that I could spend more time with 'our little problem'. After observing him and talking with him, I noticed that he responded best when actually shown visually what he had to do. I took two photos of him on the digital camera, one of him sat working quietly at his desk, the other of him sat with all four chair legs on the floor and him listening to the teacher. He helped me to process the photos and print them out. We pinned them on the wall directly in front of his desk and I find that (for the moment anyway!) he corrects his position after a simple point from me to the photographs. He also likes to be timed on a stop-watch to see how many minutes he can sit and concentrate. Each session he tries to beat his previous attempt. I am sure these approaches will not work *ad infinitum* but I shall be continually looking for other tactics to help 'Jim'.

Jim is one of the children I work with who has special needs but I strongly feel that all children are special, although they aren't all children with special educational needs. Children are all born equal and it is up to the adults around them to shape and direct their lives. They spend a huge part of their day away from home attending school, so it follows that teachers and support staff have a big part to play in developing their eventual personalities. I like to think that I am approachable and understanding and try to include consistency as one of my qualities. Through working with children with special needs I have come to question whether inclusion at all costs is the right approach, I have been able to reflect more on this over the last few weeks and feel it is an area I would like to explore further.

Becoming a supportive assistant

I try never to lose sight of the fact that I am a teaching assistant and I hope I never step outside that role. The teacher is there to lead and guide both her class and myself and I welcome the clear objectives that are always communicated to me. I am lucky that in my school the teaching staff are always open to suggestions and comments. Sometimes I get to know individual pupils better than the class teachers do, through close daily contact and can offer a way forward. I feel the teachers and other professionals in the school respect my views and ideas, as I do theirs. I am always ready to be corrected or criticised and feel that this is all part of my learning and professional development. And the teachers would, I hope, agree that we have a working relationship of mutual respect and regard.

Living and working in the community, I naturally come in contact with lots of parents of our school children. I like to feel that they see me as friendly and open although, obviously, I am always discreet about things that happen in school. I hope that if I overheard parents talking about me, one word they would use would be: approachable. They may, in fact, use many others! Some parents often find it easier to speak to a teaching assistant or learning support assistant than they do to the class teacher and many little problems can be sorted out that way. Obviously I would always report such conversations to the teacher in a sensitive way.

Looking back over my fourteen year career as an LSA, I realise that initially I must have picked up things as I went along. I started as a general assistant, working 6.5 hours per week and my very first job was sorting out the map cupboard! Not very stimulating, but I think in those days, teachers didn't really know what to do with me! I photocopied, covered books, cut paper, tidied and made tea until that great day when I actually worked with a group of children. Gradually my strengths were recognised and I was encouraged to take on more and more academic activities. I greatly enjoy science and art and the teachers are glad that I offer support in these subjects.

I was involved in local cluster training for teaching assistants and came into contact with other general assistants from nearby schools, even though this early training was in things like first aid and playground management. At my school, the support staff were always included in in-service training (INSET) days and so my knowledge grew. In 1977-98 I embarked on the Specialist Teaching Assistant course. This proved to be brilliant and my confidence and range of teaching techniques have increased enormously. Many more courses are available to teaching assistants these days, and I am anxious to take advantage of as many as possible (within the monetary constraints of the school!).

So I hope I can continue as I am, learning all the time. I would be quite happy to finish my working life as an LSA but hope that this specialist role (whether it's called teaching assistant or whatever...) is properly recognised for what it is – a valuable and respected part of the school community.

So: Why do I do the job I do?
When some days are just so grey
'Thanks Miss', 'I've got it' or 'That was good'
That's all they need to say!

Points for Reflection and Action

- Lin, like other LSAs in this collection of stories, tells us about the difficult times. Whilst LSAs support children (and their teachers), this work can be emotionally very demanding. What do you think a school ought to be doing to offer effective support to LSAs themselves?

- Gaining, and retaining, confidence is identified by Lin as an important aspect of her own personal development. What are the things that give you confidence in your work as an LSA?

- Lin says she hopes she will never step outside the role of an LSA. In your reading of her story, what appear to be the key elements of her role?

12

Klaus' story: the experience of a retired professor of special needs education

Klaus Wedell

While working in successive university posts, I was usually able to do some work in schools in order to keep my feet on the ground. So when I retired to the country, I offered my services to the local village primary school. Retirement has been rather busy, so I have only been able to commit myself regularly to one morning a week. In the five years I have been giving voluntary help, the school has usually had about thirty-five pupils on roll, grouped into two classes – rising fives and infants, and juniors. The teaching staff consists of one full-time teacher, a teaching head and a part-time teacher.

Each of the two class groups spans three to four age cohorts. In the younger class the teacher has a part-time learning support assistant to help, and the older class is shared between the teaching head and the part-time teacher. We currently also have a part-time LSA to help in the older class. For the teachers, meeting the diverse learning needs of children in each of these groups requires Houdini-level flexibility – and teaching challenges never envisaged by those designing the national curriculum and the literacy and numeracy hours. For a good deal of the teaching, the two classes are split up into subgroups, and this is where our two LSAs take particular responsibility. We are fortunate that our school is in a rural Education

Action Zone (EAZ), through which additional funding is provided for LSAs, and also for their further training.

The teachers decided that they would like me to help by supporting individual children who were not making the progress expected – mainly in literacy. Some of the children I have worked with have also had help from the SENCO during her weekly half-day visit (on different days), and some just have me for support. We have a shared SENCO who works across our pyramid of four primary and one secondary school – all with small numbers on roll. The five schools fund her between them, and the time she spends in each depends on the number of children who need help.

Two forms of support

It seems to me that support basically takes two forms. There is help, firstly, designed to enable children to take part in the normal curricular activity in the classroom – which already covers a range of levels – so that every child benefits from the teaching and learning going on in their group. This support is geared to help children to understand and respond, and so to bypass their particular learning difficulties as far as possible.

Secondly, help is aimed specifically at supporting children to overcome particular difficulties. Clearly, there is no hard and fast separation between these two forms of support. Even in our classes, which incorporate such diverse learning levels however, there are a few children who teachers feel need additional help targeted specifically at their particular learning needs. There is considerable controversy about whether this kind of help should be given in the normal class group or by withdrawing children. In our school, children already experience a variety of subgroup and whole group learning, and so 'withdrawal' becomes a relative concept in terms of numbers, particularly as the school design is partly open-plan.

Working with individuals

I've usually been allocated to individual children whom the teaching staff feel need specifically targeted help. When I first started at the school, I was assigned children from one of the larger age cohorts at the upper infant level. Most only needed help for a year or less, until the teachers felt that they could continue to make progress with their age peers. In the last two years I have been assigned a couple of children in the top year who are still having difficulties. I've emphasised to the teachers that I'm working to them, and where relevant, also to our SENCO.

When I'm asked to work with a child, I ask the teacher to tell me as specifically as possible whatever he or she would like me to help the child achieve, which the child is not currently achieving. Similarly, with the SENCO, the question is how I can support a specific need as set out in the individual education plan (IEP). The SENCO and I share a notebook in which I write down each week what I have been trying to work on with the children, and the idea is that the teacher also reads this. In a small school like ours, it is usually possible also to talk briefly with the teacher during the course of the morning. My aim is to ensure that the children are not handed to me to carry out some supposedly beneficial activity which is not a part of the teacher's own day-to-day plans for the children.

I've been very concerned that working once a week with children lacks the intensity required to achieve an appropriate rate of progress. It has always struck me that it is unreasonable to suppose that, in most instances, this kind of drip-feed can be an effective way of helping children to progress. And yet it is probably still one of the most common ways in which help is offered, largely because of limitations in staffing. I've tried to devise arrangements by which this problem can be overcome – with greater or lesser success. One of the main ways of achieving some continuity is to devise activities which the child can continue in the current classwork. In my work with the two children in the leaving class (year 6), the teacher has asked me to support them in developing their narrative writing for SATS, so it has been relatively easy to link what they write with me with their writing in the classroom. Work with children in the infants class has usually involved me in devising activities which can be carried on as part of the current classroom work, which the children can share with other children. I've also tried to organise work children can do at home with their parents for a short period on three or four nights a week. This too has met with variable success.

Focusing on strengths and needs

All through my work, initially as an educational psychologist, and later in university posts, I've been trying to find ways to focus teaching on children's particular strengths and needs. I've tried to work out how one can achieve a progressive understanding of these by starting with activities which are as near as possible to the day-to-day learning problem. If teaching in this way doesn't work, I regard this as an indication for focusing more on underlying difficulties. Not surprisingly, I've sometimes been told a child I'm working with has indications of dyslexia. I've not found such descriptions more helpful than detailed information about exactly what difficulties the child is having in the classroom. When you are an LSA it can be quite hard to get specific information about what the teacher finds a child can and cannot do – and under what conditions. It is usually more difficult to obtain information about what a child can do than about where the child is failing. There is a similar problem about discovering the particular situations in which a child performs better than in others, so as to get an idea about likely teaching approaches. These values are a subject of the initial – and ongoing – conversations with the teachers and the other LSAs.

Two main strategies for support

There seem to me to be two main strategies for working with children who have particular learning difficulties. One is to start working at the level at which the children are achieving and work up from there. This usually seems to be effective with younger children. For older children, where building up self-esteem and confidence is crucial, such a strategy can seem rather demeaning. So it is better to find a way of enabling them to achieve as near as possible to the expected level, but providing all the cuing and support this requires. Progress then takes the form of systematically removing each of the forms of support, so marking steps in the children's progress.

One ten-year old I was asked to help was one of those children who have difficulty in setting ideas down in writing. He also had some difficulties in sorting his ideas out. However, he was highly knowledgeable about sheep, and so we decided to write a booklet about what happened in the life-span of a sheep. He dictated this account into a tape recorder over several sessions and then played it back to both of us. Not surprisingly, the syntax and vocabulary of his oral account was infinitely more sophisticated than in his usual written work. We discussed the structure of his account stage by stage, making changes where necessary to improve the sense of what he was saying. He then wrote it out section by section, partly in the sessions and partly at home. I learned a great deal about sheep – for instance that barren sheep were termed 'empties', and that when you take your sheep to a show, you bring them in the night before to 'calm them down and tart them up'. The boy became increasingly impressed with his own account, so we were able gradually to omit the tape recording stage and proceed straight to writing. The complete account was finally printed out as a booklet and the headteacher helped him to incorporate pictures of sheep, so he could present it to his parents for Christmas.

Another older boy was reluctant to speak into a tape recorder. When he started at school, he had been quite disturbed, and was only gradually coming out of himself. By the time I was asked to work with him, he was much more adjusted but still vulnerable. He also had great difficulty in putting his ideas down in writing in class, although when one was able to get him to talk, he had plenty of ideas and a good vocabulary. The school had acquired computers linked to the Internet, so I was able to pair him up with an email pal in another school, as a way of getting him to see that ordinary communication could also be written. He was good at setting up the email system on our computer, and I became his secretary, typing out his messages. His progress took the form of my becoming a decreasingly competent secretary, leaving out punctuation so that he had to put in the full stops and capital letters and the paragraphing. He also had to review his writing, to consider whether he had made his message comprehensible. For me, one break-through came when he spontaneously interrupted a piece of his dictation to ask whether I thought he had explained something sufficiently clearly.

The younger children I was asked to see were frequently those at the upper end of the infants class who were having difficulty in catching on to phonics. One problem was finding out exactly which spellings they were having difficulty with. It became apparent that we needed to derive a spelling progression from the Literacy Strategy and use it to check both which aspects they had already mastered and which might be appropriate to learn as a next step. The errors the children made were usually of the plausible phonic alternative (PPA) type – which typically became apparent when they tried to spell words with vowel digraphs such as 'ou', 'ai'. Planning help for these difficulties pointed up an interesting difference of view between the teacher and myself. She thought it best to teach children digraphs by grouping words according to the various ways of spelling the same sound. My view was that the children's errors were already PPAs, and that one needed to start by teaching contrasting sounds. The contrasts needed to be highlighted by focusing attention on what the words looked like and also linking the spelling with the meaning of the words. So with respect to these particular children we agreed to differ.

Work on spelling at this level lent itself well to having children work in small groups or pairs so they could play phonics games. I had to devise tailor-made activities, adapting Happy Families games so that the families consisted of sets of relevant words with contrasting vowel digraphs the children had found difficult. The children could take these sets of cards back into their classroom, where they could teach others to play the game, and so gain kudos. I also used the computer so they could build up words with the relevant digraphs, and complete sentences using the words.

Checking progress
A crucial aspect of the 'building up skills' approach is recording progress over the short-term. The children – let alone I myself – needed to know that these approaches were in fact meeting their learning needs. Checking the accuracy of spelling words is relatively straightforward within the activities of giving individual or group help. Getting feedback about the children's performance in the classroom can be less precise – another instance where close collaboration with the teacher pays dividends.

Checking progress on the work in the narrative writing task with the older children also has its problems. In one sense, the 'reducing cues' method can be self-validating. If the children can maintain the performance level when the cues and help are progressively withdrawn, there is reasonable evidence that learning has taken place. However, agreeing for example, whether children have demarcated sentences appropriately, is more subjective, I worked with a boy and a girl who also still had limited spelling competence. We decided that the SENCO would tackle the spelling. The boy had difficulty using the given SAT title as a stimulus to start writing, but the girl wrote endlessly and with little relevance to the set title. We again used a cuing approach, largely to bypass the spelling limitations of the task. In this instance we used the Clicker software, which also spoke the written text back so the children could listen for where sentences might end. Because this work was closely geared to the work the children were doing in the classroom, the progress monitoring was largely taken on by the teacher, in the context of the assessments in the class. One could not fail to reflect on the fact that the national curriculum assessment procedure was pushing teaching into the SAT task as an end in itself.

Tuning in to children

The account of my work as an LSA shows what many of us find – that LSAs have the opportunity to tune in to individual children's feelings and attitudes to an extent which is often not open to teachers. Some children open up in conversation about their personal problems and about their family issues. Children's story writing also often reveals their preoccupations and concerns, so that one cannot help but become aware of the background to their problems. The dilemma then is in deciding how far one should allow these topics to open up, and when to make it clear that this kind of communication needs to be channelled back to the teacher. As an LSA, one at least has the opportunity to try to tune one's interaction and relationship with the children in a way which matches their needs. In some instances, children try to test the limits in terms of control; in others, one is faced with the task of defining the limits of personal inter-action. Both situations can prove quite demanding for both male and female LSAs, and it is interesting to note how the perceptions of the relative roles of child and LSA gradually come to be established over time. This was brought home to me in a tangential way when it was decided one year to decorate the annual governors' report to parents with the infant children's pictures of the staff. My depiction featured me peering intently at a computer through my half-moon glasses.

Continuing to learn

During my jobs at universities, I also tried to keep my feet on the ground by learning from the experience of the teachers on our advanced courses and working with them on their assignments in schools. I used these opportunities to match the strategies for special needs teaching with the more theoretical issues which underpin one's actions. However, I feel the recent years of work as an LSA have taught me as much again – and I am continuing to learn. The experience has also brought home to me, even more, the super-human intellectual demands made on individual teachers and LSAs faced with meeting the diversity of learning needs in class groups of children. It really is time we moved away from the rigidity which this organisation imposes on the education of our children. The contribution LSAs can make is slowly becoming recognised as part of the way in which the nature and levels of learning needs can be served by the nature and levels of expertise that a range of professional approaches can offer in schools. But as recent research into the function of LSAs has shown, it seems there is still a long way to go in many schools, before the resource LSAs represent will be fully realised. Perhaps paradoxically, small village schools faced with finding ways to respond to the complex learning demands of their multi-age classes may well be indicating the way ahead.

Points for Reflection and Action

- Klaus identifies two forms of support in his story. Which do you think best serves the learning needs of the children you work with? To what extent does such support depend upon individual needs?

- The strengths and needs of the child, according to Klaus, have to be used as the focus for intervention. How far can the LSA become actively involved in this process?

- Talking to children enables us to gain deeper insights into their world. Klaus suggests that LSAs are uniquely positioned do this – but indicates that there are some inherent difficulties. What issues do you see as potentially arising out of such an LSA/pupil relationship, and how can an LSA best deal with them?

13

Julie's Story: you just don't walk away

Julie Pester

My name is Julie Pester. I am 38 years old, married with two children aged fourteen and twelve. That just about sums up my family context. But if it wasn't for my two children I don't think I'd be writing this account of my work, because it was down to them that I started working with children in schools in the first place. I'll explain more about that later...

I went to a local comprehensive school and gained 6 GCSE '0' levels in various subjects. I was always interested in working with children and did my work experience in a local nursery. When the time came for me to see the careers officer about my future, he advised me against becoming a nursery nurse as he said nurseries would be closing and that there would therefore be no jobs. I took his advice and worked in an office... but it was a decision I always regretted.

This was put to right about fifteen years later when I started working in my children's school as a school meals assistant. At long last I was working with children! I then went on to work with special needs children on a 1-1 basis in mainstream schools, and eventually started working where I am now, a special school for boys.

You don't just clock off

It is difficult to give specific reasons for why I do this job. There are just so many of them. It's a job I enjoy and a job I feel I am very good at, but you just can't call it a job. A job is something you do between

97

9 and 5 o'clock. Working with these very damaged children, you just don't clock off at 5 o'clock. You often find yourself taking things home to do or working through your lunchtime to get something finished, and if a child is in distress you don't just walk away because your time is up. I know I'm not alone in thinking this. The various courses for LSAs I've attended have taught me that there is a huge band of dedicated people out there doing exactly the same as me.

My current role within the school is very satisfying. I have recently completed the City and Guilds Advanced Learning Support Certificate; the teacher I work with decided I needed to put my new-found skills to good use. As a result I plan and deliver a lesson every day. This includes a numeracy and literacy session. The class teacher oversees the whole thing and is on hand to give advice and support. In addition I am a budget holder for videos. Last year I set up a non-curricular video library, which has proved quite popular with the teaching staff and pupils alike.

What I like most about my position in the school is that I'm treated like a fellow professional by the teaching staff and as another teacher/mother by the boys in the school. This has advantages as well as disadvantages. The main advantages is that the boys feel able to confide in me. As they don't see me as the main teaching practitioner in the classroom, they often feel they can come to me with their problems or worries, and I can often sort them out. But I also have to point out to them, from time to time, that I am not their mother but a member of staff.

Another thing that gives me great pleasure is when a lesson I have prepared is well received by the boys. They know and accept that I teach every day, and if a particular lesson goes well and they have enjoyed it, they will give me feedback. This always pleases me, as I value their opinions and input.

Because you always worry...

The other side of the coin is that there are some things that concern me. I think we all do a fantastic job at our school and the staff has the best interests of the boys at heart. But when children come to us it usually means they have been permanently excluded from their previous school and I feel that, as a 'special school', we are expected to be the answer to all problems. Though we can address most of a child's needs there is sometimes a need for outside help. And that is not always forthcoming...

Another thing which is a worry to me is the apparent lack of skilled and experienced supply teachers with backgrounds in working with children who are perceived as having emotional and/or behavioural difficulties (EBD). Whilst this can cause great problems in a mainstream school, in a special school it can very nearly cause a riot! I have first hand experience of this, and I am sure other LSAs could also testify to such supply-staff difficulty.

Just recently a second EBD school was opened by the local education authority. In my opinion it was about time. I felt the children who were supposed to leave us last year and couldn't because there wasn't a school place for them had been badly let down by the authority.

Building trust... developing relationships

Returning to the positive, I can recall a large number of successes: I have been at the school for six years now, and I believe there have been many, some greater than others. For instance, there was the boy who had very low self-esteem so that everything he did was 'rubbish' or 'crap' – but he was always quick to praise other children. I worked in his class for two years and it took nearly all that time to get him to believe in himself the way I and all the boys in the class did. But eventually his self-esteem grew. He started to take lead roles in class activities, running messages for the class teacher and so on. Now he is one of the most confident boys in the class and, indeed, the school.

Relationships are a crucial part of my work, but I do feel it takes longer to gain the trust of the children I work with than it does with many children in mainstream provision. One simple explanation is that many of these children are very damaged. Some have been sexually abused and most have been abused in some way or other. Some are in foster care or are looked after by grandparents. Their main experience of adult relationships has been unsatisfactory.

The only way to build a relationship with these children is to gain their trust. To a large extent this is done by setting boundaries in which they can feel safe. We have to teach them what is acceptable behaviour and what isn't. This can be achieved by modelling good behaviour in class. The relationship between LSA and class teacher provides an excellent example. Showing the boys two adults working well together and showing each other respect, whilst having high expectations of the boys themselves, is a very good starting point.

My relationships with the teachers I work with have always been very good. I feel my role is to support the teacher in any way I can, but I also feel it's a two-way street: I should feel supported as well. I can honestly say I have been lucky with all the teachers I've worked with. There has always been a mutual respect between us. Although from talking to LSAs in other schools, I do know that this is not always the case – that I'm fortunate in having this positive experience.

One example of this mutual respect is that when I have sat in on case conferences I have usually found that my opinions are valued by the other professionals involved in the meeting. I have also engaged in conversation with social workers and have felt my input was valued. They will often say that the LSA knows the child better than anyone, and this of course is often the case!

My experiences of relationships with parents or carers tend to be limited. In mainstream schools parents frequently bring their children to the classroom so there is an opportunity to engage in conversation and get to know them. At our school all the boys arrive in the morning on transport provided by the LEA so we rarely see their parents/carers and, to be honest, even at parent's evenings the turnout is pretty poor. I have no answers to this problem, only to say that some of our parents/carers do their best for their children under very difficult circumstances.

I have on occasion spoken to parents/carers on the telephone for various reasons and am generally treated with respect. I think it is mainly down to the fact that I have a good relationship with the children and I suppose that they tell their parents that I am 'alright'.

What next?

What of my future plans? I must confess that this is a difficult one. I feel I want to go on to learn more about my profession but, to be honest, I'm running out of courses to attend! I hope to carry on with the course I am doing at the University of the West of England in Bristol, in order to gain a Certificate or Diploma of Higher Education. I know my school will support me in this.

Training opportunities are excellent at my school. As an LSA I have always been encouraged to attend any course I feel will be of benefit. This has included City and Guilds courses (funded by the school) and one-off training days at the LEA's education centre. I have also completed courses in basic counselling skills which I feel are of enormous benefit to me and the children I work with. We are all regarded by the school's senior management as being on our own personal learning curve and therefore this kind of professional development is actively encouraged.

One thing I do know is that I would not want to go on and train to be a teacher. I feel I am a good LSA. But the pressures of teaching would be too great for me. At the moment I feel fulfilled in my role as an LSA as well as my role as a mum and a wife. I think this would change significantly if I went on to train as a teacher.

To sum up, then, I am very pleased to be part of my profession and it never fails to amaze me when I encounter the total commitment of other professionals in my field. I think we are all out there doing our best for the children we work with.

Points for Reflection and Action

- Julie's story, like others in this book, raises some concerns about supply teachers in special schools. If training were to be offered to supply teachers who opt to work in special schools, what could LSAs contribute to a training programme?

- LSAs, according to Julie, seem to find themselves positioned sometimes at a point between teacher and pupil, What appear to be the inherent tensions in this state of affairs – and how could they be resolved?

- Julie acknowledges that it is hard to find an answer to the reluctance of some parents of children who experience EBD to interact with their school. Why do you think this happens? What can an LSA do to improve matters?

14

Pamela's story:
being with children

Pamela Gray

My name is Pamela and I work as an LSA in a special school. I left school when I was fifteen and went to college to take a residential child-care course. The course lasted for two years, after which I worked in a children's home. I am married and have three children of my own. I come from a family of eight children and have far too many nieces and nephews to mention! I have always been involved with children in my family – babysitting for nieces and nephews as they grew up and now even babysitting for their children.

I first got started working in schools as a parent helper in a mainstream school. A job came up that gave me the chance to work one-to-one with a child in Primary Five. I stayed working with him until he was in Primary Seven, at Easter time. It was decided that he did not need an auxiliary – a Learning Support Assistant (LSA) – as he would be moving on to attend secondary mainstream school. At this point I was offered a transfer from a mainstream school into a special school, which I accepted. In all the time I worked in mainstream school I did not receive any training that would help me to meet the needs of the child I was working with. I have stayed in special education and have been in special schools for five years now. My situation regarding training and development has changed since I have been in special schools. I now have training in the areas of epilepsy, first aid, understanding the challenging behaviour of children with learning difficulties, and with autism, and in information and communication technology (ICT), Makaton, and early communication skills. I have also attended training in limiting and managing crises. I participate fully in the life of the school and have been involved in play schemes and residential trips. The work of an LSA is not well paid and so I do a variety of other jobs outside of school too. I help out at an after school club, do some cleaning and am also a babysitter. As well as this I work in community education provision and have done so for twelve years. I am also a part-time youth worker and was an under-twelves 'development worker' for six years.

Working in teams

My work as an LSA in the school I am in now is extremely varied. I work in five different classes throughout the school and work with different members of staff. I am part of five different teams and each one works in their own way. The differences are slight, but you become aware that each teacher has their own views on what responsibilities should be given to an LSA, in comparison to a nursery nurse for example. This is interesting as a lot of the work I carry out is not too different to that of a nursery nurse – I change nappies, see to the needs of the children at mealtimes and am involved in implementing children's individual education plans (IEP). One of the frustrating aspects of being an LSA is trying to work flexibly when you are in partnership with a teacher who is reluctant to be as flexible as you. You might know a group of children well and be able to make judgements about where the greatest needs are at certain times. If you work with a teacher who is not willing to deploy you where you feel there are needs, it is easy to feel frustrated. I do have specific responsibilities in the classes in which I work and these generally relate to the computers. I am involved in setting up and moving children up to new levels in the spelltime literacy work and I am regularly involved in word- processing work with the children.

I have acquired many skills since I have been working in this special school. Many are technical skills and I am called upon to use them quite often. Not all the staff in my school are fully up to date with the technological age! So I am often asked to use the camcorder or digital camera or do certain things with computers. I have also learned to drive the school minibus. This has its advantages and disadvantages. In the past, there have been times when few drivers were available and out of necessity I was often exchanged from one class to another so that I could drive the minibus for them.

Supporting parents

I enjoy working with children in both mainstream and special schools. Their abilities might be different but this does not affect my enjoyment. In my time as an LSA I have found that some parents are not always as realistic about their children as they could be. My view is that a child should be allowed to be a child; wrapping children up in cottonwool can cause problems. For example, some parents do not especially like to see their children out in the playground running around, just in case they fall. If there are medical reasons, this is understandable but if not, it can be very frustrating because you will have seen those children running around laughing with glee.

While taking their difficulties into account, I think it is important that children do learn right from wrong. If a child kicks other children he has to learn how to stop. The parents have to be involved and have to consider how society looks upon their child's behaviour. If a parent thinks their child should be allowed to do as they please, it causes problems in working with that child in school – as you have to consider how a child's behaviour will affect other children in your care. You have to think about their safety. This is why it is very important to have a policy for working with parents. My school has such a policy. This can be very advantageous to the child because it means that the school and the parents can really work together to help the child develop to the best of their ability. It means that we can meet the children and parents in their own environment and I have enjoyed making home visits, usually in the evening. It is always useful to see the child in his or her home environment as you can look at how they are behaving with their parents. Their behaviour at home may not always be the same as in school. I have been surprised when a parent came to the school asking for help with the behaviour of a certain child at home when we found no behaviour difficulties in school. In a situation of this kind you cannot just wave a magic wand to make everything better, much as you would like to.

Schools can only do their best to give advice and then check to see if it is working but we can not live in the house with the family and offer help in this way, which in some cases might be what could help everyone. Children often display different skills and abilities at home and show a different side to their personality. Likewise they can sometimes do things at school that do not seem to transfer to home.

Enjoying the children

I enjoy working with the staff in my school, especially their willingness to help each other with anything. Staff will ask me for assistance and I feel that I could go to them and ask for help if I needed it. Although there are times when I feel frustrated in my job, the whole school ethos is excellent. Anyone who comes into the school to work or visit is always made to feel welcome.

The thing I most like about my job is working with the children – if you did not enjoy being with children there would be no reason for working as an LSA. The kids are the biggest motivator for me to do my job. The relationship you have with them is so important. I feel that they feel secure with me and there are times when they want to share some very personal things. I try to help them to feel secure and comfortable by having a laugh with them but I also balance this with firmness so that they know where their boundaries are. My greatest satisfactions in my work are all based around the children and the progress they make. It is a real success when a child learns something new or achieves a new level when I have been working one-to-one with them. It can be the slightest thing that makes you feel that successes are happening – such as a smile, or eye contact – and it gives me a real buzz. It makes the whole job worthwhile.

Future plans

I get a great sense of enjoyment from my work as an LSA but my future plans include continuing to look for other jobs – leaving LSA work completely. This is nothing to do with the nature of my job but all to do with the money I am paid. The school understands that this is the situation and I am supported in looking for employment else-where. I have to do lots of extra jobs to earn the money I need to make ends meet and a higher salary would mean that I could reduce the amount of extra work I have to do. I love my job very much and do not want to be in a position where, due to the need for a better salary, the day comes when I have to leave. That would be a sad day.

Points for Reflection and Action

- Pam's story demonstrates that she has to work within various teams in a flexible manner. What would you see as the key personal qualities that are required for working in this way?

- To what extent can/should an LSA support those parents whose children who are presenting difficulties at home but not in school?

- Pam closes her story by honestly explaining that the pay she gets as an LSA is not sufficient to make ends meet. To what extent does such poor remuneration for LSAs affect the way that other (more adequately paid?) colleagues perceive them?

15

Amy's Story: you never get bored

Amy Hamilton

During my secondary education I didn't have any strong desires career-wise. Most of my friends aspired to be computer engineers or graphic designers but I could think of nothing more terrifying than being stuck in an office all day. As I went through various options with my career advisor I always ended up returning to the caring or teaching professions. With something to aim for, I embarked on a course in Health and Social Care and Ethics but I was unable to complete the course due to personal problems. I decided I needed to experience the real world. I moved away from Bristol and became a Community Service Volunteer and have never looked back. My professional life, involving supporting individuals with physical and mental health issues, had begun.

Five years later and back in Bristol, I came to work in a hostel attached to a residential school for children with severe learning difficulties. The school followed the philosophy of Rudolph Steiner and I became curious to learn more about such outlooks on life. I was pleasantly surprised by the ratio of staff to children: for the first time I could actually care for, rather than just manage, people. All in all this seemed a very warm working environment and so when the position of class assistant became available I felt I needed to move on to this greater challenge and expand my experience.

At present I work alongside a special needs teacher and three other classroom assistants. The children in our school are aged between six and nineteen and I am directly involved with a class of six to twelve year olds. There are seven in the class. They have disabilities ranging from Rett syndrome to autistic spectrum disorder to cerebral palsy. Most display emotional and/or behavioural difficulties (EBD) and all bar three are in wheelchairs. Because our children's basic human needs are so great, our roles can range from feeding, to nappy changing, to assisting the physiotherapist, to having inputs to literacy and geography lessons. Oh! and not forgetting being involved in encouraging the children to express themselves: the children cannot communicate verbally!

I am not sure whether separate special schools are a help or a hindrance with regard to inclusion or whether they contribute to the continuation of labelling. But I do believe we have the advantage of specialist advice. Thus my job is made more effective by having on-site speech therapists, occupational therapists and physiotherapists. We have regular visits from educational and clinical psychologists. We can also ask the advice of specialists in particular fields who might, for example, travel from Germany and spend time with the school, offering fresh ideas to support tour work with the children. I feel our SENCO is an asset and is always on hand with support when we need time out – which we quite often do as our self-esteem and morale can often plummet. I believe that we have adequate resources in comparison to a mainstream school but I also believe that you can never have too much support, especially when you consider the diversity of needs we have to cater for!

One of the things I really like about this job is the fact that you can be in the class with a child exploring sensory equipment one minute and the next you could be in the hydrotherapy pool or horse-riding. You never get bored, as there are always areas in which you can educate yourself. I have always had a particular interest in autism and what better place to learn more about it than here. Moreover, I feel you learn so much about yourself personally and this can only be a good thing. How many jobs allow you to enjoy being able to incorporate work and play!

I get total job satisfaction when I see these children experiencing 'normality' in their own way – getting covered in dirt and mud in the playground, or interacting with their peers. Years ago they might never have left an institutionalised unit. But as well as these feelings of satisfaction, I have just as many worries and concerns about teaching children with special educational needs.

Challenging my thinking

Part of my role, as an LSA is to help children meet certain levels of attainment. Most of the class I work with are within the Key Stage 3 age-range. But their cognitive ability is a very different matter. Most will never reach Key Stage 1. They will stay at pre-level 1 across most areas of learning. Some of the children have severe developmental difficulties. This is just one issue for the teacher and LSA. Just how are you supposed to teach a class whose developmental range is so broad? I ask myself: how much do the children benefit from a curriculum of maths and science? I believe they need to be stimulated in so many other equally important ways, such as sensory work, to recognise they have a body they can use! More attention definitely needs to be paid to tactile learning aids and Makaton so that the children can communicate effectively. We need to try and get inside the minds of these children if we want to truly understand and help them. Individual Education Plans (IEP) can seem so time wasting when you think realistically that many of the children will never live independently. So isn't it more beneficial for them to leave our school with as many self-help skills as we can teach them?

In our teaching situation, what we call success may seem trivial to others, but the activities and experiences we place emphasis on are often the things people take for granted. For instance, I recollect working to get a child to press the button on a recorder so that musical notes would play, thus demonstrating cause and effect. It took a week for the child to accept me using a hand-on-hand method without biting me, and another two weeks of constant verbal prompting until they understood the concept. Another child had a similar highly specific target to aim for; he had to recognise which story we had been exploring for literacy. Again, progress was slow but eventually he could show us by his eye movements or gestures that he did know what we were asking of him. As regards milestones of achievement, examples like these really do constitute success stories for us.

Being part of a team

Our school believes that rhythms and routines are extremely important to the children. They provide a form of security; many children live in their own self-absorbed world and we strive to bring them into the world that surrounds them, so that they can interact with others. For things to run smoothly any changes to routine need to be introduced gradually. Conventional teaching methods need to be adapted in very particular ways. For the children to engage in work effectively they need to get hands-on experience. For example water and flour can make dough: the children need to taste and touch and do whatever they feel necessary within an acceptable frame. If they are prevented from doing this everything will be far too abstract for them to understand.

Everybody has different ways of teaching and they need to be respected even if theirs is not the same approach as the one you favour. Differences in opinion can cause friction amongst staff and I am glad I have not experienced this at first hand. I know of cases where LSAs are seen as mere dogs-bodies and domestic supporters, whose responsibility stops at putting on coats at the end of the day. The way in which a teacher perceives you is a vital part of our work and negative feedback can make it impossible to work alongside some teachers. Thankfully, my experience has been that most teachers value your support in the class and see you as an active contributor with an intellectual role.

I have personally had a lot of experience of working with autism and challenging behaviour before I became an LSA and I know this has greatly helped me in facing issues in the class I currently work with. Professional development continues to be very important. So although I feel that I have had a lot of training days such as those on non-aversive handling techniques and on Makaton, they do not go into enough depth to really be put into practice effectively. Training is a tool which can help us to help others and I think that more money should be spent on training for LSAs in particular. We do have brains, you know! This brings me neatly on to my expectations for the future...

I plan to advance as much as I can in this job! I don't want to stay being an LSA forever, yet at the same time I don't want to become a teacher. The work just seems to be endless and is always being updated and just as you have got used to one method, along along comes another. I would, on the other hand, like to be involved in a more specialist area such as speech therapy. After all, education covers such wide scope – as I have discussed. Why not start in communication? Where would any of us be today without this vital skill?

Points for Reflection and Action

- Amy notes that every teacher seems to have a different style of teaching. To what extent can the same be said for LSAs? What challenges do these different ways of working pose for an LSA?

- Amy clearly sees her previous work experience as an asset in her work as an LSA. Can you recall particular experiences about which you could say the same?

- Amy talks about the role of special schools in her story. Do you think that the work of an LSA differs according to where s/he works? Or does it depend on the individual needs of the child?

16

Christopher's Story: being an object of reference

Christopher Swann

My involvement in SEN has only been for three years. The vast majority of my working life has been spent in the commercial sector, predominantly in a sales environment. I had reached a point where I felt less in tune, and no longer comfortable with the underlying value system of the industry I was working in. Near where I live is a residential school, which I was aware of through friends and personal contacts. I approached them to see if there was a position available where I might use my existing skills and be of benefit to them. Three hours after I had talked to them and looked around the school, I received a telephone call to ask if I knew enough about computers to become their ICT Co-ordinator. I spent an initial period visiting each class on an observational basis, to see if we were happy with each other... and stayed.

I am not sure that there is an easy answer to the question 'why I do this job?' I know that at a younger age I would not have had the inclination and, perhaps more importantly, the patience to work with children with severe learning difficulties and challenging behaviour. It did occur to me that, on one level, I had a desire to fulfil a personal wish to belong to an educational system I value, albeit a specialised offshoot. Overriding this however, is the challenge of being able to make a difference, sometimes only temporarily, in the quality of life of the pupils we have in school.

Pleasure and satisfaction: ICT and PMLD

I work as ICT Co-ordinator three days a week. I work with around twenty children on an individual basis, who have a one-to-one session each week. Because many of the children at school have PMLD (Profound and Multiple Learning Difficulties) and/or challenging behaviours, very few of these sessions specifically involve literacy, although numeracy and literacy can be augmented into programs for a few pupils. One pupil can be given simple dictation and enter a diary using a Writing with Symbols program and a concept keyboard. For many of the others, ICT can provide an experience of cause and effect, improve concentration and promote hand-eye co-ordination. Motivating children to activate these programs can be simply a musical reward or animation at the end of a picture building sequence. Programs are accessed by touch screen, switch or mouse, and overlays for a concept keyboard can be customised to enhance picture-word association and reinforce symbol-sign recognition.

I am also involved in running an afternoon indoor games session. Because of the wide range of ability among the children, and the fact that each has a carer with them, it is also quite a challenge to come up with activities that all can be involved in to the best of their ability.

Many things resulting from working at my school give me pleasure and satisfaction. The fact that an ICT session involves something that looks like a television, has animated images and sound effects or musical accompaniment puts me in the good books of most of the children. This obviously helps when I collect a child from a classroom for my session. Hearing a child laugh and smile after seeing the results of a completed sequences on a program is a delight. Laughter is one way to help build relationships, and although acknowledgement one day by no means guarantees the same response on another day, it never fails to bring me pleasure.

Feedback from another member of staff, reporting an improvement in a child's mood or concentration following ICT work, is also nice to hear. Colleagues generally communicate well and support each other, which creates a positive environment in which to work. I feel that the children and young adults resident at the school are lucky to be surrounded by so many caring and committed people. It makes for a stimulating atmosphere and it feels like a privilege to work there and be a part of these young people's lives for the time they spend in the school community.

Although many staff members are dedicated to the care of the pupils, there is also a fairly high turnover of staff. The reasons for this are varied, but younger carers and LSAs often leave for better salaries and less stress elsewhere. Volunteers come and go and the overall effect can lead to a lack of continuity for the children. Because of their disabilities, our children benefit from routine and a rhythm to the day. Frequent staff changes can create uncertainty and feelings of confusion for some children. Our tight financial budget also means that resource shortages are a frustration. Making comparisons with some other schools' resources makes me wish that our children had access to a wider range of experience in some areas than we can give them.

Success and change is hard to record in most of our children. With some children it is about maintenance of the skills they have, as in the case of a girl with Rett syndrome – a neurological disorder, so far found only in females, that results in regression of previously learned communication and physical skills. For some pupils the ability to make choices by eye-pointing to a symbol or indicating a particular picture is an achievement. One example of success is that of a young boy who, when I first started working with him, would just randomly keep hitting the switch that activates a picture building program on the computer. Over time he learned to stop pressing the switch at the completion of a sequence once the picture had been animated and wait for the signal on the screen to start building the next one. This may seem not to be much of an advance but, when seen in the context of his level of disability and the number of sessions it look to reach that stage, I see it as quite a leap forward.

Relationships

Building relationships with the children is one of the most important and rewarding aspects of the job I do. Many children with autism, for example, do not initiate social interaction, For them, making a successful connection with somebody is especially gratifying. A few of the children only associate me with their participation in an ICT session. And when I collect the children from their classroom, I become for some an object of reference. One problem people with autism have is a resistance to change and one way of helping to overcome this is for the child actively to want to take part in a particular task. If there is an association between me and having fun, then there is a good chance that we will get off to a good start. There can be a down-side to this, however, in that some children have a tendency to become obsessed with screens, be they television or computer. I have found the best way of approaching this is to give plenty of warning that everything will be turned off after a specified time. Then I count down the number of input actions that the child has left. It doesn't always work, but it does remove the worry element for them of an activity coming to an abrupt halt.

Although not specifically structured, there are spaces in the day when all teaching staff and LSAs have opportunities to spend at least a short time exchanging information. Before the school day starts, we have a short meeting where staff absences are notified and details of how these will be covered are given out. Any vital issues we should all be aware of concerning specific children are talked through. This start to the day brings everyone together and is, I think, one way that members of staff build good relationships. Because the children return to their hostels for lunch, staff have time to eat together and talk further. There are, of course, situations that make communication more of an effort. Part-time staff and therapists have to make sure that they are up to date with events, and must actively seek out information. Nevertheless, the culture of the school is such that forming relationships and links for communication are encouraged.

Our school is a residential special school, so teaching staff have much less contact with parents than they do in mainstream schools. The hostel staff have more regular contact, talking to parents when collecting or returning those children who have an occasional weekend away. Staff have meetings with the social worker and parents of each child every few months to discuss issues and exchange information. I see one or two parents a year if they are visiting and want to see ICT facilities or discuss software for use at home during holidays.

There is on-going staff training, usually on INSET days. These focus on a range of things: manual handling of children, Makaton workshops, communications aids and symbols and so on. I have recently completed a two-year course for a Certificate of Higher Education in Care and Support of Pupils with Severe Learning Difficulties, funded by the school, in association with the University of Plymouth.

I have no specific long-term plans but expect to remain at the school for some while. As I gain more experience and knowledge, I would like to feel that I am a useful resource to the teachers, and a facilitator for enabling the children I work with to develop in their learning as individuals.

Points for Reflection and Action

- Like Christopher, many LSAs have considerable experience in other jobs. To what degree do you think this is either helpful or incidental to an LSA in their work?

- Christopher has assumed the role as his school's ICT co-ordinator. What do you consider to be the advantages and tensions – for an LSA – in undertaking such levels of whole-school responsibility?

- Christopher talks about 'making a difference' to the learning experience and quality of life of his pupils. How do you think an LSA knows that they have made such a difference – however small this might be? How would a pupil know?

17

Karen Simpson's Story: 'this is where I want to go'

Karen Simpson

I currently work in a pupil referral unit (PRU) for children at Key Stage 3 whose behaviour has resulted in them being permanently excluded from mainstream schools. My official title is behaviour support worker (BSW), and I work both in the unit and as an 'outreach' worker, assisting in the reintegration of pupils.

Starting out

I was a nanny for seven years and got made redundant so... I just needed a job! I was next on the supply register in my local area and was asked if I would go to a comprehensive school to do some supply work. I stayed for four years. It was a county school with an inner city catchment. A lot of the kids were quite aggressive... a few of them were, anyway. But on the whole it was just a normal comprehensive school. But I loved working with the 'naughty' ones.

Most of the children I worked with had MSG (Mainstream Support Grant) and there was one particular girl who had ten hours worth of support. She was a typical EBD pupil, if there is such an individual. I absolutely adored her and when she left I was bored and thought, this is where I want to go...

But no jobs ever came up. Then one of the outreach teachers in the pupil referral unit (PRU) told me there were some jobs coming up. 'They're going to be PRU-based, do you fancy it?' So I came to meet the deputy head before the jobs were advertised to see what it was going to be all about and decided, yes! I *would* like it. But all I knew at that point was that I was going to be PRU-based, working with KS3 children who had all been permanently excluded from school. I then had to wait for the jobs to be advertised, but when they came up they were only for a two-term contract, and temporary. I was already on a permanent contract. But I was disillusioned and needed motivating, so I took the risk and applied for them. And that was it really, I just needed a challenge. And I liked the challenge of those sorts of kids in the comprehensive school, so I decided to go for it!

I suppose I just don't like 'normal' young people. I know that it's not a very good reason or a very good expression to use! My husband thinks I'm absolutely crazy and doesn't think I get paid enough for doing what I do, especially when you consider the hassle we get. But every day is a challenge and these young people really need help, and I want to be the person to help them.

The job is such that I take most of it home. I can't switch off – which is a fault – though in some ways it's not a fault. A lot of the kids we work with are looked after (in the care of the Local Authority) and you do build strong bonds with them, though of course not just the looked after ones. Sometimes you just can't switch off – it's not like a normal desk job where you do your paperwork and then go home. You're dealing with kids' emotions here, and its difficult...

The challenge of challenges

My current role has so many features. The job was originally intended to be PRU-based but I work as an outreach behaviour support worker (BSW) a lot now. At the moment this is a key feature of my work: supporting kids and preventing, or helping to prevent, kids from being excluded. In addition I do a lot of work with other LSAs, supporting them and offering them strategies and suggestions about how to manage behaviour.

I prefer to be out and about rather than in the PRU. Fortunately I'm PRU-based only on one day a week, Friday, and this is for outdoor education! Generally, if I'm not in schools then I'm in the PRU. When I'm working there it's more like supporting the class teacher and not actually being pro-active. It's a bit like fetching and carrying, so I think this part of my role needs defining a bit more. We need to work on that within the PRU. I do feel that I'm more challenged when I'm out in schools. In a way I feel that is where I am more useful – but that's just my personal opinion.

To illustrate: when I am working in the PRU full-time and start the process of reintegrating a (PRU) pupil back into school, I can easily be told to 'fuck off', because kids become so familiar with you: they know exactly what you're going to do, how you're going to react. I think you've got more authority if pupils see you coming in to just have a quick chat with them. I feel there should be someone (other than me) who is PRU-based and who doesn't do the reintegration bit. I could then still do the reintegration because they'll know who I am, but they wouldn't get too familiar with me. If you work with the pupil in the PRU your relationship can break down if that pupil didn't fit in to school, or if they weren't achieving as you'd wanted them to or would like them to... So there's a tension between you needing to really get on with the kids but also needing this space in order to deal with this kind of thing.

Another aspect of my work is delivering a lot of training. I really enjoy that. It was hard when I first did it. I remember the first time at a national conference. I was petrified! But I've now done five or six more. I've done the LSA conferences and I really enjoy that, because of contacts with the other LSAs and going into schools and seeing and helping them.

It's not just about me getting ideas across to a wider audience, it's more about me learning from other people, so it's a two way thing. It's nice because we did some training of special needs co-ordinators last week and afterwards we actually got some phone calls! For instance, 'Can you come in and just observe this kid to make sure we're on the right track?' And you go in to the school and this helps to reinforce to them that they *are* doing it right and that nobody can wave a magic wand! So we learn off each other and that's really useful; it is good to meet up with people from different schools. I could possibly imagine myself becoming a trainer... *possibly*, but I'd still want contact with kids. I'd still want to do some work with them. I would like to do more training work, but at the moment it is important that I get the balance right.

High points, concerns and frustrations

I like working on a one-to-one basis with kids, just getting to know them. I love being out and about with them. I especially enjoy the outdoor education programme in the PRU, and I regret that I've not been able to do any this academic year yet. When we did it last year what happened was interesting. I'm absolutely useless at climbing and stuff like that and one of the kids actually taught me to climb – which was great for their self-esteem. It was awful for me because I got stuck up an 8ft. wall and I couldn't get down, but he (the pupil that is) talked me down! In spite of these adventures I really do like the outdoor education bit. I'll do anything with them, I just enjoy being with them.

A lot of things cross my mind when I think about the work I do. At times I worry about my personal safety and that of my colleagues. Some kids can just flip – just like that and there are no warning signs. Then there's times you know you've got a kid in the PRU who schools won't take on account of their behaviour, and yet you know that they can achieve academically and socially. And then you see that they're actually ready for the reintegration but because the school is stalling and stalling and stalling, you see them deteriorating and in the end being damaged. They've been here too long and it's not our fault... that really upsets me because I know that a lot of our kids can get back into mainstream schools and would be successful but they're not being given the chance It's not our fault – it's just the system.

I don't think that the kids come to us too late. But I think that once they've been permanently excluded from a mainstream school and we've worked with them for some time, we do reach a point when we're doing an 'integration readiness scale' and they show us signals that they're ready to go back to school. But the schools aren't always ready or willing to take them at that time, and the longer they're here, in the PRU, things can get worse. It's rather like when these kids first arrive here, most of them get worse. It's normal really! I mean, its not really my role to manage the integration. But in some of the schools I know I will go in and say 'I've got a lad...and what are you going to do about it, blah, blah...?' And we've got kids in quickly sometimes that way. All of us do that. But we can't push their buttons any quicker than that. It's frustrating, but there's not a lot I can do about it to be honest. It's beyond my remit, unfortunately.

But we've had a lot of success. The one that comes to mind is a young man who was reintegrated into his school. I supported him in his first few lessons for each subject.He did maths first, then I'd withdraw after a couple of lessons. Then he'd do English or whatever. And after about a term he was in the school for four mornings' three a week on his own, though with school support obviously. Next he went on the activity week with school and was OK with that. By the September he was in the school every morning and I was able to withdraw. He was fine! But it was very, very slow. Just adding sessions. I mean, now he's only in two full days and three mornings and that's a year later. But come September he'll be in full time. It's more important to do it gradually. And although I withdrew, the key teacher is still there. So mine is just the first bit. Getting him into school, getting him used to the environment, working with him, telling him where he needs to go...and just being a bit of support for them. He's a success, he's doing really well. It's great, it boosts *my* self-esteem, but I think it boosts all of us because it's not just me doing it! It's the team in the PRU as well, and all the work the teachers have done with him. It's everyone. It's a team effort. I just finish it off.

We were lucky on that occasion. The school this young man went into is a very inclusive school. They've got a good special needs support team and were willing to take it slowly, as we were. Some schools aren't like that. They worked with us – we worked together and the key teacher (from the PRU) is still working with them.

All this takes a lot of time. I just used to go in for the first hour each morning. But the first hour soon becomes two hours with the travelling between the unit and the school. So it's time-consuming at first. At the end of the process it was just me going in to meet him before he went into registration. I was a familiar face – we still care about you, we're still here if you need us, you know where we are, and so on. And that's all it was for three weeks. Just two or three times a week, popping in to see that he was OK. That was enough but, as I say, it is very time consuming.

Getting on with people

I relate to the kids in a similar way to a teacher, but obviously I've not got to deliver the curriculum. So my role's a bit different. I'm very fond of them. A lot of the kids see me as a teacher but I sometimes tell them that I'm not. But they just respect you as a teacher, so I've got quite good relations with them.

I think they're a bit more open with you, though, when you are based in a mainstream school – this was how it was when I was an LSA in the comprehensive school. But my role is *nothing* like that of an LSA in a comprehensive. I go in to the school and the kids see me as a teacher. It's up to me whether I choose to tell them and sometimes I do and sometimes I don't.

I think that the kids also need to see you on their home territory. I mean there was one pupil I'd previously done two observations on at school. Then I went on a home visit at 6 o'clock at night and he didn't even know I'd been watching him! But I told him that I didn't want to be introduced to him in school, I wanted to be introduced on home territory so that he knew I was there to help *him* and work with his Mum and Dad. Because at the end of the day we're there for the kids. Yes, to support the school but mainly to support the kids in achieving, in succeeding and we'll do whatever we can. If it means going and doing home visits, then so be it.

As regards the schools, sometimes I don't even tell them I'm not a teacher. I just go in and say 'Hi, I'm Karen, the Behaviour Support Worker...' and they don't know whether I'm a teacher or not. I try to use that to my advantage sometimes! I'm not saying this about teachers, but if some of them found out that you were LSA or something like that they'd start talking down to you...talking to you as though you were an idiot.

Fortunately that sort of thing is not quite so common now, because the schools I work in think I can go in and help them, wave the magic wand! But I was fortunate in the comprehensive school I used to work at. My SENCO was wonderful and so were most of the teachers. There were the odd few who thought I was a fetch-me – carry-me person. And student teachers used to say, 'can you photocopy me this, can you photocopy me that', because they didn't actually know what the role of the LSA was. But in the PRU, it's quite the opposite. I am one of the staff, the core team and that's it. In schools, they just want help and if you go in to help they're eternally gratified to you and praise you and want anything you can give them. My role is different to BSWs at other PRUs, who don't do as much outreach work as I do, though I'm not a hundred per cent sure. But I do a lot of outreach work. It's a strength for me so I think they're using that and challenging me all the time.

I also have a lot of contact with the parents. If I'm going to organise the reintegration of one of our pupils then I'll do a home visit, and I'll contact them every week, once a week. It's parents *and* carers: I've done some work with a kid both in school and the unit and I've only been contacting his carer and visiting her. So I've got good relationships with parents – yes. As I say, I contact parents every week, regarding the 'cases' I'm working on. For instance, there's one young person I'm working with at the moment and I've done a session at home with the parents, just to build up a relationship, to support *them.*

Parents and carers see me as Karen the BSW. I don't think they actually know what my role is. I did a home visit with Ray (head of the PRU) the other week and he just said to them that Karen is one of my staff from the PRU. So they just see me as Karen. And I will tell them what my role is and what I'm going to be doing to set up a behaviour support plan. So they actually know.

We'll always – that's Ray and Joan (head and deputy head of the PRU) – do a risk assessment. They'll know the family anyway. If I'm going to do a home visit they'll say 'Are you confident about doing that, Karen?' I did a home visit at six o'clock at night, for example, and Joan said 'Stop there for half an hour, do what you've got to do then leave'. But she'll ring me half way through to make sure that everything's fine. So they do have a lot of confidence in me but then I think I've proved myself over the last 18 months.

Dealing with stress

If we've had an incident we all have a fag – because this PRU has got more smokers than any of the other PRUs. I also go shopping, shopping therapy's pretty good! Or I go home, have a bath and have a drink. Or I go out and have a *really* good drink! When we've had a really bad incident I go home and go straight to bed.

But we always have a de-briefing. I can't talk it through with my husband because he finds it hard to understand what my job really involves. He doesn't think we should have to put up with the crap we do. But that's his opinion ...he's great, but I can't really talk it through with him. I have a really good friend who's a teacher who works for the City Behaviour Support Service. So if I'm really stressed she comes round. So it's difficult for my husband because all I really want to do is sit there and blurt it all out.

But when I have an incident in a school and I've come back in the PRU I feel really proud of myself, because I've held it together. But then I come back into the PRU and see Ray... well, not Ray, because crying in front of your head of unit is just a nightmare. But I see Joan, his deputy, and I just go to pieces, and break down. But they talk you through it, they support you. The support I get is brilliant. If we've ever had any incidents everybody phones each other at night to ask 'are you alright? Is everything OK?' So we all have to be a support to everyone in the team. Of course, not *all* staff phone each other and ask if everything has gone alright, but most of us do. The thing is, I had an incident with a pupil and I knew I had to go back to the school the next day. But they said 'You don't have to go. That's fine. If you don't want to go that's not a problem'. But I went, because I wasn't going to let a situation like that beat me. I won't go off sick. We worked out today how many days I've had off in the thirteen years since I left College – six days!

Looking to the future

I've done a course with the Association of Workers for Children with Emotional and Behavioural Difficulties (AWCEBD). But I've not actually got that many qualifications. I've got my NNEB and also done a special needs assistants course. In addition, we've had lots of

INSET with the Service, on literacy, numeracy and other things. I've got a big wallet full of all of the things we've done. I'm also doing my counselling skills Level One course. But I don't know what else I want to do because there's not that much out there to do! Lots of teachers say to me, 'Why don't you train to be a teacher?' But I don't want to be a teacher. When they say that to me it makes me feel that I'm undervalued in what I do. And if I train to be a teacher who's going to do what I do? Because someone's got to do it.

But I don't know what I want to do in the future. I thought I wanted to be an educational welfare officer (EWO) but I don't know about that now. There's not that many courses out there, to be honest. I've done my AWCEBD course, and there's nothing to move on to really. There's a Diploma, but I don't feel comfortable about doing that because of the content. But there's not much else really for me to look at. My LEA have done a pack for LSAs, training courses, but there's nothing in there that takes my fancy to be quite honest – there's nothing that jumps out!

The reason I did the AWCEBD course was that I was going to learn something from it, I was going to learn something that would be useful in my day-to-day work. I was talking to an LSA yesterday and we were discussing these new job descriptions being brought out by the County and discussing which pay-scale we would go into. I said that for the top of the scale you have to be very well qualified 'Well, I have an HND', she said, and I thought 'God, I'm dead thick because I haven't got an HND or anything like that. But I don't see the point in having a piece of paper for the sake of it. I could go and get a degree but if it's not going to be useful to what I'm actually doing I don't see the point. I need something that is relevant to me doing my job now.

In the job I choose to be in I'm top of the scale anyway. With the new job descriptions that are coming in I could be on the top one if the service decided to have a senior post – that is if the draft ones that I've seen go through. If the Service decided to have one and it goes to interview I don't know what will happen and what they'll decide. A lot of LSAs or BSWs within our service haven't got an NNEB or Btech or an NVQ3, which all represent qualified status. We once had an LSA who was a qualified teacher who got paid unqualified rates, so I really don't think that qualifications are relevant in this job – so long as I've got my NNEB I'm qualified. So, at the moment I don't know where I'm going. I'm thirty-two and I've got plenty of time to do stuff.

At the moment I'm being challenged so much. If I've had a crap week, Friday just can't come quickly enough. Personally and professionally I'm being challenged that much. But it's a team thing, and at the moment I'm quite happy. I look through the job pages every week, but who doesn't?

Points for Reflection and Action

- What different skills and qualities does Karen have to make use of in her relationships with a very wide range of people – pupils, teachers in schools, unit staff, parents etc?

- Karen tells us about some of the ways in which she manages work-related stress. What strategies and provision do you think should be available for LSAs (and teachers) working with children who present challenging behaviours?

- Do you think it is necessary for LSAs to have formal qualifications? Why or why not?

18

A collected story: LSAs in conversation

Tim O'Brien and Philip Garner

One of the ways in which we obtained the views of LSAs was during a series of group meetings. These were convened in three locations. We or a colleague from high education or from an LEA acted as facilitator and chairperson. The discussions were built around the themes we had identified during our planning of this work – the identical themes to those used in our discussions with individual LSAs and as a 'framework' for their written accounts. Each discussion lasted approximately 45 minutes, was audio recorded and subsequently transcribed.

In all over sixty LSAs, mostly women, participated in these discussions. But the full cohort represented the widest conceivable range of backgrounds, levels of experience and viewpoints. In this chapter we provide some illustrative extracts from these data, based on five of the key themes the LSAs discussed:

- their background and early educational experiences

- their reasons for deciding to work as an LSA

- features of their current practice

- their successes

- their worries about their job

In keeping with the overall spirit of this book, though, we keep to a minimum our outsiders' encroachment on the interlocution: what these LSAs have to say, in common with those presented elsewhere in this book, warrants scrutiny and carries significance in its own right. Our only compromise has been to identify those issues which seem to us to be made apparent by the illustrative extracts we have assembled. We have highlighted these in italics at the end of each set of LSA comments.

So what we provide here is a series of indicative observations which point to the tensions, challenges and (in particular) the opportunities face by LSAs at the present time.

1. Background: family context and early education

- Being a parent yourself was the best training to have to start with. It's the best training you can get because being a parent yourself, you can understand children. You know how to approach children.

- It also helps you to deal with the parents. As a parent yourself you realise there are anxieties and worries with all children and I just think you can deal with them on a parent-to-parent level. You can certainly empathise with what they're going through. I'm a parent and I worry about my children and they worry about their children.

- I left school and I wanted to be a teacher but I lost my nerve at the last minute. I then applied to go to college to do something else

- I didn't enjoy school I wish that when I was at school it was like it is now.

- When I was at school I used to help some of the kids who were not as clever as me – I was good at that as I was a clever child. It's strange, but now I do it as a job.

- I hated my primary education but secondary school was quite good for me.

- I absolutely loathed being at school. I'd cry and just didn't want to go. In those days (not so long ago I suppose) there wasn't the explanation that you'd get now for new children in school. You just went and got on with it. And there wasn't the support and the real breakdown of everything you did that you get now, with these literacy and numeracy hours... it just wasn't like it then. I'm very surprised I've gone back!

- My Dad said to me 'I can't believe you've gone back!'

- My Dad was a doctor and my brother and sister were really good at school. Maybe in some way I rebelled and did not want to be like them... I don't know... I have never really thought about it a great deal... but now I really make an effort to try to help children understand that school days can be happy and you only get one chance.

- Your bad times make you think about things now. When I hear a child say 'I can't do this!' I home in on it because you know exactly where they're coming from.

- It's easier to empathise with their struggle because you've been there before. You know exactly what is going on in their head, don't you?

- There's lots of good memories that I can go back to. I was really happy in school, especially in primary. I'd spend ages playing at school with my two brothers, though I don't think I ever thought I'd end up spending a large part of my adult life working in a school.

- Sometimes you hear a child tell you that they hate being who they are... and you think... I have been there... and I can help you get out of there.

Commentary

Learning Support Assistants, like other professional groupings involved in education, bring with them a range of background experiences – and not least those which relate to their first contacts with formal education, as pupils in schools. As with teachers, their recall of these early encounters with 'learning' in its widest sense can have significant impact on their future practice as LSAs. Thus, in the extracts we provide in this section, it appears that these LSAs are using their recollections of their own school-days in one of two ways.

On the one hand some of the LSAs report a fairly negative experience as a pupil, and even express surprise that they have chosen a career which takes them back to the 'scene' of their unhappiness. One explanation for this may be, in the words of one LSA: 'I remembered school, especially at primary, as not a very happy place. I hated some of my teachers. And when I started, or was thinking of applying for this job I just thought – 'I can do better than that'. *The cathartic outcomes of returning to a setting that holds and provokes memories of personal unhappiness in order to make the situation better for others can be a strong motivational factor.*

A second effect of early schooling on an LSA's practice stands in marked contrast to this: that the very experience of being a pupil themselves enables them to have insight into why some children struggle academically and socially. So here the LSA is using their own experiences to identify with a child's 'struggle' – this we see as connective empathy in action.

But it is equally apparent that LSAs do make use of their wider experiences as parents or carers. Many of those who have contributed to this book acknowledge, in the words of one, that 'having been a parent I know what makes kids tick, and I'm in a good position to talk things through with them – at their own level'. *On the other hand, very few of our respondents made mention of other occupational experience – a state of affairs explained in part by the fact that many are women whose professional careers have been interrupted by the responsibilities of parenthood.*

2. Why have you chosen to work as a learning support assistant?

- I started purely as a helper... because my children were in the school and I had some free time and I was asked if I could help out in the classroom... that's how it starts... a bit of reading, a bit of painting. I enjoyed it so much that when a position became available and I was asked if I would like to you know... do it as paid, I jumped at the chance.

- Because there is an element of job satisfaction and I wouldn't do it if I didn't enjoy the work.. .you do it because you enjoy it.

- One of my closest friends had a child with special needs. I remember how she got hardly any 'congratulations' cards. I felt her pain. I think I decided then and there that I would, when I got the chance, go and work with children who have special needs. Five years later I became an LSA.

- I started out as a helper. The school didn't have any LSAs at all when my sons went through and then they advertised a 6-hour job that I... That the head said to me... because I was a helper there... you might be interested, there's something coming up. I was interviewed with two or three others and got the job and over the years the hours have gradually increased until now I'm full-time.

- For me it was because one of my daughters only had a year in school. She died when she was six, but she was so attached to the nursery nurse in her school that I could see what a valuable job she did in the school and what a help she was. I just want to give something back.

- I answered an advert! Why? Because my children were grown up and it was time for a new challenge!

- Why do I do this? It fits in with me at home, because of the children.

- I'd not do another job, I enjoy it so much. I never had children of my own, so I suppose you could say they're a substitute, although I don't consider that to be the case when I work with them

- I left the police force and wanted to carry on working with juveniles. Working as a classroom assistant seemed an ideal job for me as I had no training in education but had a wealth of experience of enjoying working with young people. I was not too sure how it would go down if a man applied for the job – but it has turned out to be perfect.

- I really enjoy what I do and don't want to change it at all. I know I could be better off somewhere else, but I feel valued. I am one of a team; I feel that they listen to me as if I'm important!

- It is convenient for me at the moment. It's convenient because I've got a child who's still in the school and I've got no-one to have them during school holidays so it's a very convenient position for me to be in. I don't have to find childcare or things like that and the hours are very suitable for me.

- It's not a job that I think 'Oh God! Monday! Here we go again...' I really do enjoy it. And I feel most of the time that I'm giving something back to the children I work with. You don't get results every day. But occasionally you do and that makes up for all those the days when you don't get things back.

- I've been doing this job for about 14 years. I can't see myself doing anything else now. I really do enjoy it. Even on bad days there's usually something... If you've had bad days with the children the staff have given you a laugh or something. If one of the staff has got on your nerves a bit there's always someone else to talk to. It sounds silly, and you're probably all going to shout at me, but during that six week (summer) holiday, towards the end of it, I'm quite ready to go back to school.

- I always worry about them in the six week holiday – especially the special ones.

- I work with children with emotional problems, some of them come from very poor families, and I always worry about how the children will cope with Christmas. I think about them on Christmas day and hope that they are OK.

- We have a 50% turnover of children every year. None of our children who start out in Reception end up in Year 6. They're here one day and gone the next! During those six weeks you often wonder what's happened to them and where they are.. and if they're alright. I hate going away!

- We really do get attached ... there's not many people that can say they go to work and they get attached to their job.

- I can't understand those people who yearn for early retirement. That's not something I've ever thought about. I think it (SEN work) is in you, it's instinctive. I suppose it keeps you involved... you know.. it grips you... in the best possible way.

- I've done this job for a long time now and I like it, love it. I get worried when we talk about whether or not we'll close down. I couldn't do the job anywhere else...oh no...never. It's something with me...I'd be unhappy in any other place...I'm sure of it.

- You give everything to the job... even though we are not paid according to the work that we do... what other job could I enjoy as much? I love it.

- There wouldn't be anything other than this work that I'd want to do...not really totally involved like I am with this.

Commentary

Our reading of the data presented by all the LSAs we have talked to indicates that they offer three rationales for their choice of career. Whilst just one of these appears in some instances to be the major influence on their decision, for the majority of LSAs each of the three hold some importance.

Firstly, then, there is the pragmatic explanation – that working as an LSA enabled other responsibilities (mainly family) to be attended to. For some LSAs this 'convenience' element appeared to offset the low rates of pay and low status. There are suggestions, at various points in the stories we have included in this book, that the 'pragmatic' rationale is of considerable importance in their strategic decision-making about a career.

On the other hand, several contributors suggest that certain events act as 'triggers' in prompting them to become LSAs. Such triggers can include recall of one's own schooling or a specific family or family-related event or incident. To this group we would also add the wish, expressed by a number of the LSAs in this book, to pursue a career which gave them job satisfaction.

A further explanation comes in the form of serendipity. Some LSAs talked to us of just 'drifting into becoming a volunteer helper' in school and then being presented with an opportunity to formalise this involvement as a paid worker.

3. What are the key features of your work in school?

- I work with a small group. I wouldn't feel comfortable working with the other children... just my small 'group'. They're my little workers... everybody knows that!

- I think we act as the bridge between parent and school; parents want to come to tell us things that they would not particularly want to say to a teacher. They worry that the teacher might think they're being silly about it. But they will come in and tell us.. so, we're the bridge really.

- I was taken on for a statemented child, so I'm not funded by the school. I'm funded by the child's statement, although I'm not necessarily working only with that child. You normally work helping others. For example, when 'my' child is away I will still be in that class helping other children

- It's nice to work with just one child.. but it's also nice to work with groups. I'm not really sure which way I prefer it...

- To support teachers and children...I actually teach everyday.

- I used to only work with the younger children... then the head-teacher said that we had to move around and work with different age groups – he talked to us about it, but really he had made the decision. I was very worried about working with the older children. That was a few years ago. Now I am grateful that we were moved about because now I feel confident going into any classroom in the school.

- We're usually working outside that classroom so it leaves the teachers free of five or six of the possibly most 'difficult' children. Although I might be trying to help a particular child, there are also three or four others who are equally challenging, and it's really hard isn't it?

- Working with a group can be harder than working with the whole class.

- We always get the chance to discuss with teachers beforehand what they expect of the session and what they expect of us in particular.

- We plan the IEP with the teacher. Because we mostly work with children who require an IEP we perhaps obtain more 'inside information' than the class-teacher.

- We tend to be given a copy of the IEP to scan through, and asked 'Do you agree with it?' or 'Would you look at it and give us your opinion on it?'

- Sometimes when the teacher is away, me and another LSA will take the class.. for the whole day... teaching the children... but we don't get a teacher's pay for that day!

- We are asked if we want to be there at parents evenings to give our input because we work with that child more on a daily basis than the class-teacher does

- In my school we have weekly meetings with the SENCO and the LSAs together and we are able to share any worries, concerns or general information about any particular children.

- I work with the pupils who are finding it difficult to be in class... in a special school that is... I work with them outside of class to try to get them back in again. It's tough at times.

- We are part of a team. We've recently got a new head and we thought it would change but we're such a strong team that she's keeping us together. We do get a lot of say, I must admit, and if there is something that we have a problem with we can go and see her.

Commentary

A number of features are highlighted by LSAs as descriptors of their work in schools. One is struck by the range and variety of duties that they undertake; these span involvement in the formal, taught curriculum as well as social interactions. In the case of the former, LSAs have become important contributors to the literacy hour in schools. Our conversations also suggest that, in some schools, far from being 'assistants', LSAs are assuming teaching responsibilities for groups of children – and in some cases reported to us, for whole classes, when the teacher they mainly work with is either present in school or absent.

Involvement with IEP – writing is seen by many of the LSAs as an essential aspect of their work – they sensibly point out that, such is the nature of their involvement with individual children, they are frequently best placed to make these inputs. They said rather less about their role with regard to individual behaviour plans (IBPs).

Great emphasis is placed by these LSAs on teamwork and upon 'relationships'. Indeed, these two aspects of their work could be said to be the defining motif of their work. Teamwork is clearly of significance in respect of their relationships with teachers, and there are also indications that these LSAs regard their involvement with parents as being crucial to their role.

4. What are some of the successes in the work that you do?

* I like it when you actually see the child's face when they accomplish something that they haven't been able to do for a long time. All of a sudden it clicks. That is the reward at the end of the day. You have your bad days but the good days help with the bad ones and it's just so fulfilling to see that they have achieved.

* Success for me is enabling the child to do something that they probably wouldn't do if they were just left to get on with things on their own.

* If I had my time all over again I would probably have become a teacher, knowing what I know now. But on the other hand, I really enjoy my job now because I've got the good things without the terrible responsibility of all – of the homework marking and all the after-school preparation and planning that they have to do. I've got a small part of that, but I can go home at the end of the day and obviously leave all that behind – whereas the teacher is working all hours of the night sometimes.

- I once cried when a child I was supporting made the sign with her hand to tell us that she needed the toilet. I can not explain what a breakthrough that was. It changed her life... her dignity I mean... It just reduced me to tears. I was happy and proud.

- We are never left out or anything. We're part of it all – an important part.

- We're always treated with great respect.

- I think it's great when the ones who have left see you around the area, they always say 'Hello, Miss...'

- We see both sides of the coin. We see what's going on behind the scenes and sometimes I think that teachers themselves find that quite valuable, when we can say 'Well, this is how it happened.

- I just like listening to the children, They talk to me and they tell me everything and they trust me. They share everything ... they are so trusting. They do rely on me and I just.... I quite like that.

- Some of the children would definitely rather talk to me than ask the teacher – that feels good.

- Where I work (a secondary school) some of the children with SEN really struggle because of the difference from their primary school. They just can't cope with the difference. They have so many different teachers ... five or six each day. And so we've started supporting their emotional needs from this September onwards, with just one teacher and us (the LSAs). We went in during the summer and painted the room. We've made the area just like a primary school classroom, so there are displays everywhere – it's all cosy. The children come in at break time and lunchtime, playing Monopoly and things like that. We're actually turning people away now, which is a shame. The atmosphere is primary-school in ethos, and the children act quite differently there. This is one of my successes.

- We once had an assembly and secretly the deputy head had gone to all the children before this assembly and asked them what they liked about the LSAs. He then made certificates for all of us and suddenly presented them to us in front of all the children... they all clapped and cheered. I had to go up to get mine... he read every one of them out aloud... I can remember all of mine! It said, 'We like the way you help us to grow up, to behave better, your kind words, the way that you listen to us and your laugh'. I was so chuffed... look, I'm even getting emotional now talking about it... I still have that certificate at home.

- I think it's nice when they come back to school to visit, I've been in this school for 16 years, and the other day a young girl came back to show me her baby. It's nice to think that they remember that you're there and they come back. They still feel that they can come in and talk.

Commentary

The LSAs we have conversed with often 'quantify' success in an intuitive and personalised way. Often their interpretation of 'success' is located around the 'small steps' made by a child on the way to mastering a skill and around the more social aspects of their school experience. This observation in no way suggests that they are indifferent to the routine or official evaluatory mechanisms that schools are required to adopt.

Much is made in these data of the nature of LSAs' contact with children – of listening to what children have to say and valuing the feedback they receive from them. That these pupils, many of whom have significant learning difficulties, complex cognitive and sensory needs and often some deep-seated emotional scars, feel able to talk quite readily to LSAs is, we believe, cause for celebration.

5. What are the things that currently concern you about your job?

- I feel strongly that classroom assistants are still classed as paint-mixers, with the wage scale to match. Yet now we're expected to do a lot more... we're even expected to teach!

- We do go on lots of courses, often in our own time and we probably do as much work as the teachers for very little pay.

- Sometimes I think we're more up to date than some of the teachers in our school.

- I would like some recognition for the training I am doing, you know, given respect for doing it and sharing it with others.

- There is a big responsibility put on you and at the end of the day if you haven't delivered the goods... the buck stops with you, though I know that the teacher has the ultimate responsibility. We're lucky in our school because nobody would ever dream of actually saying 'You haven't done this or that today'. Within ourselves it does make you feel very responsible though.

- One or two teachers seem to look down their noses at me – as if to say 'I'm much better than you'.

- We don't get enough time to plan what we're going to be doing in lessons alongside the classteacher. This is not making very good use of us.

- There are times when I worry about job security.

- I get concerned about the pressure on me to become a teacher, to be honest. I like being an LSA, and they seem to be saying 'You'd have more respect if you were a teacher'. What does that tell me about their opinion of me as an LSA?

- The biggest pressure to me is that I don't know whether I will still be supporting my small bunch of children this time next year. It all depends on money, and LSAs are the first to be made redundant when a school has money trouble.

- I would like the government to finally decide whether we're valuable or not. If we are, then we should be paid in such a way that it represents the value of the work we do.

Commentary

Both internal and external pressures are at work on LSAs at present. The former include status and rates of pay, coupled with the paradox – currently so apparent – that LSAs are seen as pivotal to the quest to secure more widespread educational inclusion. Financial concerns, too, are never very far away; for many LSAs this brings great uncertainty, given the widespread use of short-term contracts linked to the requirements specified in statements of SEN.

Internal pressures include the impact of increased level of stress amongst educational professionals. As with other groups, LSAs do get affected by change and by external pressures on schools, both of which have been endemic features of the English education system during the last ten years, where changes have been numerous and rapid and consultation has been conspicuously absent. And whilst they are insulated from some of the most obvious stressors, there is nevertheless a knock-on effect in many cases.

In some schools, regrettably, LSAs are still regarded, and shamefully treated, as second-class citizens – by the teachers who would un-doubtedly benefit from the enhancement of the role, status and pay of this group of workers. And so, while training opportunities for LSAs will undoubtedly assist in developing their existing skills, they will only be fully beneficial if they are accompanied by a parallel programme of professional development of all other staff in schools. Such a programme, it would seem, needs top focus on the role of the LSA as a bona-fide, committed and active contributor to the learning of all pupils and to the life of schools as organic and inclusive learning communities.

19

The Researchers' Story: some notes on the process of collecting 'untold stories'

Tim O'Brien and Philip Garner

This collection of stories was obtained from learning support assistants working in a variety of geographical locations in the British Isles. Over a period of about twelve months we invited LSAs to construct accounts of the work they did. Our data is opportunistic, in that this invitation was given (a) to LSAs we met as a result of our involvement in school training days, (b) to LSAs who were following long-courses in a number of Higher Education Institutions (HEI) with whom we had professional contacts and (c) to LSAs we knew personally through our own partnership work in schools. In all over 80 LSAs were invited to offer contributions. The request for 'stories' was not underpinned by a specific wish to secure narrative accounts from LSAs who were working in particular settings or who had particular backgrounds. Our intention was to make connections and see what happened, admittedly informed by a reasonable expectation (based on our own contact with LSAs) that there would inevitably be a wide range of viewpoints, experiences and backgrounds represented in these 'stories as data'.

But it would be inaccurate to suggest that these stories have been elicited from a group of LSAs who are, broadly speaking, homogeneous. At the outset we did have an intuitive feeling that there would be some quite striking individual differences and we sought, up to a point, to plan for this. Thus we were keen that our invitation to contribute should include approaches (for example) to LSAs whose views might be influenced by their own

- personal life-histories

- experiences of education as a pupil

- professional experiences in other settings

- cultural and social values

In the stories we collected, these influences invariably overlapped, although at various 'moments' in the professional lives of these LSAs a single issue may have assumed dominance. But consideration of these factors always remained as a secondary determinant in identifying which stories to include. To us the impact of the narratives themselves was the principal consideration.

In arriving at our selection of individual stories for inclusion in this volume we have tried to apply a general, overarching criterion: is the LSA telling a story which offers the reader a new or alternative insight or perspective into their work? Little of what LSAs have written has to the best of our knowledge been published before, so we could assume that all these accounts would in all probability represent a new and refreshing commentary on this aspect of special educational needs (SEN). But we were also guided in our judgement by the question 'Would the reader find this story informative for the development of future practice?' Indeed, one of the reasons we decided (after considerable discussion) to add a series of 'Points for Reflection and Action' to each of the chapters was to identify a set of issues which, we believe, will be of some significance in the professional development of LSAs and teachers.

The accounts contained in this book have been obtained in two principal ways. Firstly, LSAs were asked to write, in a reflective manner, about the work they currently do and the range of influences on the way they operate. It was left for each LSA to decide whether they wished to work to a structure within a loose 'writing frame' (see below) or to write in a more personalised, unstructured way about issues affecting them. It was emphasised that what we were aiming to secure in both cases was a series of stories in which the voice of the LSA predominated – rather than a set of quasi-academic accounts, complete with technical references and appropriate linguistic conventions. The latter, we argued, could be obtained elsewhere, since the increasing body of literature seems to be *about*, rather than *by* LSAs.

Secondly, those LSAs who did not wish to write in the ways described were invited to participate in a semi-structured interview, based around the key topics contained in the 'writing frame'. These interviews, which lasted for approximately 30-35 minutes, were audio-recorded with the permission of the LSAs concerned, subsequently transcribed, and then returned to the LSAs for verification of the accuracy of their story as they had told it. In some cases, more than one semi-structured interview was carried out so that concepts and contexts could be further explored, clarified and grounded.

In addition to the story-gathering procedures described above, data were also obtained through a series of focus-group discussions, also audio-recorded and transcribed, in which six to ten LSAs discussed the issues identified in the writing framework. The format of these sessions, which lasted for about 45-50 minutes, enabled interaction to take place *between* LSAs: in many cases it was apparent that they used these sessions to clarify, via discussion, particular points of tension or potential relating to their practice.

The framework used in each of the data-gathering approaches represented an opportunity for LSAs to comment on ten areas or aspects of their work. Information was sought on:

- background: family context/education

- rationale for doing the job

- nature of current role in school

- things I like

- things that concern me

- success(es) I can recall

- relationships with children in school

- relationships with teachers and others

- training opportunities

- future plans or expectations

Our gathering of data, quite apart from being undertaken according to agreed ethical guidelines defined by various organisations (for instance, BERA), was conditioned also by the belief we both had – discussed in more detail in our *own* story in this book – that the voice of the LSA was sacrosanct as 'data'. It was with this undertaking in mind that the LSAs agreed to talk with us. We believe that our position as practice-based, and hopefully action-based, researchers, would be compromised if we began a manipulation of the data, thereby altering the meaning and intention of the words originally used.

Finally, we undertook to respect the confidentiality of the LSAs and those they worked with, in all matters where they indicated that anonymity was essential. Thus, real names (of children, teachers and others) have been changed in such instances; similarly, the names of the schools are not directly attached to each story. The stories were seen again after editing and approved by the LSAs, who then sought and obtained permission from their school or other place of work for its real name to be included in the list of acknowledgements. The wishes of any LSA or school who felt unable to agree to publication were respected from the outset.

Index